# SHETLAND DIARIES

# SIMON KING

## SHETLAND DIARIES

### OTTERS, ORCAS, PUFFINS AND WONDERFUL PEOPLE

HODDER &
STOUGHTON

First published in Great Britain in 2010 by Hodder & Stoughton
An imprint of Hodder & Stoughton
An Hachette UK company

1

Copyright © Simon King 2010

The right of Simon King to be identified as the Author
of the Work has been asserted by him in accordance with
the Copyright, Designs and Patents Act 1988.

A CIP catalogue record for this title is available from the British Library

Hardback ISBN 978 0 340 91874 6
Trade paperback ISBN 978 0 340 99874 8

Typeset in Monotype Sabon by Ellipsis Books Limited, Glasgow

Printed and bound by CPI Mackays, Chatham ME5 8TD

Hodder & Stoughton policy is to use papers that are natural, renewable
and recyclable products and made from wood grown in sustainable forests.
The logging and manufacturing processes are expected to conform
to the environmental regulations of the country of origin.

Hodder & Stoughton Ltd
338 Euston Road
London NW1 3BH

www.hodder.co.uk

For Marguerite
The adventure continues

# Contents

# Introduction

This is an account of a love affair with a place and its people. This relationship started with dreams and matured into a reality that exceeded all expectations. The life journey that brought Shetland into my consciousness and compelled me to meet and get to know her more intimately is the framework of the tale that follows.

The content of my conversations with those I met along the way has been paraphrased and abridged to give the essence of the exchange rather than pedantic detail. I hope those whose words I have adapted will forgive me. Events are relayed in a chronology that is broadly accurate, though I have taken liberties here and there with the timeline to help with flow and to avoid repetition.

I have had the extraordinary good fortune to live and work among people who have not only welcomed me and my family to their home with a warmth, honesty and humility that is humbling, but who have also been instrumental in introducing us to many of the astonishing events, natural and man made, we have witnessed. Many are named within these pages, and it seems churlish to single any out. But I'm going to anyway.

My heartfelt thanks go to Helen Moncrieff; RSPB warden, leg-wrestling champion, first-class naturalist, enthusiast, oracle on all things Shetland, social manager, and unsuspecting but staunch fact-checker for this book. I owe to her more than words can offer.

To John Campbell, gentleman, kindred 'otterholic' and finest field-naturalist; for so generously sharing his special knowledge built up over many years of careful and caring observation of Shetland's otters.

To Brydon Thomason, enthusiast and finely skilled naturalist, for always keeping us in the loop and sharing with us some of the most ephemeral and dramatic wild events on the isles.

To Tom Jamieson for cheerily offering the use of the Solan IV at incredibly short notice and always with a smile.

To all those who helped to care for our daughter, Savannah, when Marguerite and I were spending long hours in the field watching wildlife; thank you for making her experience of Shetland rich, fun and full of love.

And, glib though this may sound, a genuine and heart-felt thanks to everyone on the isles who welcomed us with such warmth, hospitality and honest care. Perhaps the most precious gems we have taken with us from Shetland are the friendships we have made.

Thanks too to my publisher, Rupert Lancaster at Hodder & Stoughton; for having the courage of your convictions, sometimes in the face of adversity.

To my agent, Caroline Michel at PFD, for unwavering support, moral and practical, especially when the precipice felt close.

To the production team associated with the television series, especially those who lived through many of the highs and occasional lows of life in the Isles; thank you for your company, good humour, professionalism, discretion and support.

And at the risk of sounding like a chairman at a board meeting, a few notes about the rules of the land.

We worked closely with the authorities when watching and filming the wild creatures of Shetland. Many are shy (the animals, not the authorities), sensitive and rare, and are protected by law. We had to seek license to film and follow many of the subjects featured in the book and television series and were offered advice and support both in the planning and practice of observing and filming them. Common sense should prevail when watching wild creatures, but sadly there are times when enthusiasm and lack of experience can cloud judgement. If you have any sense that you may be causing a disturbance, then it is time to move away. The list of species protected by law in Shetland is almost as long as the list of species found there. If in doubt, check.

A final word of thanks, to my wife Marguerite, who was sanguine about my love affair with Shetland and who has come to share the passion. I have often been absent, even when we were side by side, either lost in my world of otter spraint and distant diver calls or locked into the word-mine. Thank you for enduring my absence and for being there when I surfaced each time.

# Chapter 1

## Infatuation

Nothing can prepare you for the shocking reality of the moment. Though logic and learning, research and preparation have all led to this point, when the gunmetal surface of the ocean swells, then bursts, to the rising black delta of the fin, still your heart skips and you catch your breath. And as the fin rises to impossible heights, your inner child whoops and screams and marvels and chills to the incongruous, magnificent, terrifying magic of it all. Then the killer whale emerges further, his great slick back pushing more of the quicksilver sea to one side, his breath, short and explosive, punctuating the still air. And you hear your own voice, your own expulsion, which may be articulate but is more likely a grunt or a squeal or an expletive. The oceans, the unfathomable, unknowable depths, have presented you with a glimpse of one of their most precious secrets. For just a moment, a leviathan has visited your world of air and land, and, for just a moment, you have connected with it.

And then it is gone, swallowed by the sea once more, leaving only a flat pond of still water where its great tail fluke has pushed down and powered its four-tonne bulk beneath the surface.

The journey that led to this encounter did not cross

time zones. It did not require the learning of a new language – though that was thanks to the local community condescending to speak in accents my English ear could penetrate. It was a journey that began when I was still in my teens: impressionable, unconventional and searching for a focus for my passions. As with so many teenage infatuations, the subject I homed in on adopted the status of an idol. But unlike most it was not a person, not an actress or pop diva, but a place about which I obsessed.

Shetland. One word to conjure dreams and hopes. Shetland – the Shetland Isles – a distant archipelago as exotic, attractive and inscrutable as any poster girl. And, as with so many adolescent dreams, the thought of meeting my idol one day was both thrilling and daunting. If left in my imagination, she could remain wild, rugged and beautiful. I would never need to know her true personality and risk challenging her perfect image.

I did finally encounter the subject of my infatuation, though it would take over twenty years for circumstance and will to lead there. I would not be disappointed.

On almost every map of the British Isles there nestles a small box in the top right-hand corner into which is crammed a string of islands. They appear ragged and torn, with names that sing of their Norse heritage, such as Yell and Unst. For most, it comes as some surprise to learn that the largest of these islands stretches over 70 miles from north to south; that there are over 100 discrete isles in the chain, 15 of which are inhabited by man, offering over 900 miles (1,450 km) of coastline to the ravages of the ocean. They are closer to the Arctic Circle than they are to London and almost as close to Bergen in Norway as they are to Aberdeen in Scotland.

Three hundred miles northeast of mainland Scotland, the Shetland Isles crouch obstinately amid the otherwise uninterrupted might of the North Sea and stormy Atlantic, their heads held low against the winds and giant waves. Their position on the planet and exposure to the elements have sculpted their profile. No towering, snow-capped mountains, no swathes of coniferous forest (the latter as much due to the ravages of humanity as the elements) but instead a hunched defiance, a stubborn protest of land in the face of an incessant maritime campaign. The hardy grasses and heathers turn their backs to the worst of the winter weather, face away from the prevailing wind, shoulders braced to the beating. Despite the near constant onslaught of wind and wild weather, the coastline is largely gentle, with gradual boggy slopes running to the shore. Sweeping white-sand beaches, rocky foreshores backed by peat banks and shingle are the norm. But here and there, goliaths of rock rise up against the storm. Towering cliffs – some grey and sombre, others pallid and sculpted like melting wax – tackle the ocean's wrath head-on. The inexorable might of the sea chips away at these stubborn protesters, leaving a few standing alone as rock towers and arches that will, in time, have their feet cut from beneath them and topple into the depths.

These waters are restless, unpredictable and cold, frequently lifted into swollen giants by unchecked winter winds that rage and scream from the southwest. They are the same seas that swirl against the Arctic Ocean; their chilled riches nourish vast shoals of herring and mackerel, and on their currents countless ships have foundered and been beaten on to the rocks. Through their core runs the Slope Stream current, whose warming, calming influence helps prevent the full force of polar conditions from gripping the isles through the days of darkness from November to March. This is not just the northern edge of Britain; the Shetland Isles feel like the edge of the world.

The disconnected cluster of rocks in the box in the top right-hand corner of my map of the British Isles was all I knew of Shetland as a young child. The same islands were barely visible on my globe of the earth – which doubled as my secret stash for unfinished Easter eggs once it had been separated from its stand and split in two along the equator. The tiny flecks of land were nothing more than a brown smudge lost in the sea between Britain and the Arctic; they might well have been made by chocolate-coated fingers pushing the planet to a close. My youthful imagination and passion for all things animal and wild was filled with visions of African plains or the frozen wastes of the Antarctic, and was largely blind to the idea that wilderness might be found much closer to home. Even as a young teenager, exploring the woods close to where I lived in southwest England, I had no real concept of what lay to the north – beyond the giant Cairngorm mountain chain, peppered by the tortured forms of ancient Scots pines. Like so many people, I had no reason to consider the northernmost hurrah of British soil as anything more than a lost and lonely outpost.

# Infatuation

It took the writing and photographs of a gentle and self-effacing man to propagate the seed of an interest that was to develop into a full-scale passion: Bobby Tulloch, Shetlander and naturalist. I first noticed his name when checking the credits attributed to photographs in books and magazines. My own interest in photography and attempts to capture snapshots of the natural world were already well established, and my curiosity to find out who was leading the way demanded that I check the creator of any image that caught my eye. Bobby's name seemed to stand alone when it came to depicting European otters in the wild. Of course, there were many photographs of otters, most set against the lush green of an English fresh-water course. But many of these, if not all, I assumed or deduced were taken in captivity. The otters in these images were portrayed so close up in frame that their enclosures were not visible, but it seemed clear to me that the wild spirit in them was somehow dimmed. They posed, fur fluffy and dry, necks stretched and eyes gazing wistfully off to one side or other of the frame.

Bobby's images of otters were different. Though some-times not as crisp and clear as those portraits taken of captive creatures, what they lacked in technical precision they more than made up for in atmosphere and a sense of wildness. Many of these otters stared at the camera lens and, as such, into my own eyes. I assumed they were aware of the photographer and were on the cusp of flight, heads held low, nostrils flared for a hint of human scent to back up their doubts. Most were sodden from a dip in the sea, their chocolate-brown fur clustered in V-shaped spikes along their flanks, giving the impression of soft scales. Some writhed on their backs in seaweed exposed by a low tide; others lay one against the other in family groups of mothers with their cubs. Few were shot at such close range that their portrait excluded the world in which they lived: this was a world of steel-grey water bordered by rust, dark brown, yellow ochre and shades of grey; the colours of Shetland. Here and there, an image would appear that broke the trend of muted tones and instead was vibrant with poster-paint vivacity: impossibly blue waters and citron-coloured reflections of distant hills bathed in sunlight. These images, together with Bobby's evocative words describing a land of Arctic splendour populated by creatures whose names rang with an exotic timbre like Arctic skuas, red-throated divers, bonxies (great skuas) and tysties (black guillemots), nudged my imagination away from the more showy natural spectacles to be found in Africa and India and towards the subtler, harder-won prizes of a land dominated by a cold sea.

When, at seventeen years old, I took the daunting but thrilling step of leaving school and embarking on a journey to try and carve out a career as a wildlife film-maker, it was in the wake of a pivotal experience alongside one of the world's leading specialist cameramen, Hugh Miles. Hugh had generously allowed me to shadow his work on one or two productions based in southern England and this privileged window into his world sealed my conviction that I should try and follow in his footsteps. During our conversations, I discovered that Hugh and I shared a love for a book that expressed in prose our own approach to watching the natural world. J. A. Baker's *The Peregrine* describes one man's winters on the east coast of Britain following these mercurial birds. His quiet, gentle dedication to unobtrusive observation, and his ultimate acceptance by the shy subject of his passion presented me with a modus operandi to which I vowed to adhere.

I continued to stay in touch with Hugh as my own career began to develop, and always marvelled at his intimate, sensitive portrayal of the world about him, which in so many ways echoed Baker's approach. But it was in the early 1980s that the stars truly lined up to ignite my Shetland obsession with a renewed fervour. Hugh had proposed to the BBC Natural History Unit a film about wild otters in Britain. Despite initial doubts from commissioners, he was given the go-ahead and set about a life-absorbing commitment to record in detail, and for the first time, otters in the wild. His advisor in the field was Bobby Tulloch. The location, Shetland.

*On The Tracks of the Wild Otter* was first transmitted in 1984. It took Hugh to Shetland over two summers and one winter following the focus of his story: a female otter he came to know well and which, in time, came to know him. I had been in touch with Hugh during the making of the film and had heard some of the stories of endurance and commitment it took to achieve his goal. The resulting film was sublime. There was no musical score, simply the sounds of Shetland to accompany the images: the wailing calls of divers and the piercing laugh of kittiwakes in summer, and always the whisper or crashing cymbals of a sea whose tempo was dictated by the wind. The narra-

tive followed a similar flow and dedication to that of
Baker's pursuit of the peregrine and was a very personal
journey of frustration and elation as Hugh tried to close
the gap between an elusive wild spirit and himself.

I watched in awe, and with a building bubble of love
for the place that had simmered in my young imagination and now was given more structured form through
the poetry of Hugh's images and storytelling. Hugh also
produced a lavishly illustrated book that told in greater
detail of his experiences living alongside wild otters in
Shetland, with photographs by himself (and a few from
Bobby Tulloch) and wonderfully free 'line and wash'
drawings by John Busby. The combination of intimate
photographic images alongside sketches that captured
the very spirit of the creatures and places they portrayed
made for a book whose pages became worn at the corners
through my constant use and reference. The very physical struggle that Hugh had had to endure in order to
gain access to the inner sanctum of an otter's private
life was daunting – walking alone for miles every day,
carrying heavy filming equipment in all weathers – and
demanded a strength of mind and body that I doubted
I possessed. A good day's work for Hugh might result
in a ten-minute roll of film being exposed. Many days
ended with no view whatsoever of his elusive quarry. His
tireless mission to reveal the world of wild otters
reminded me of two mantras he had passed on to me
when I first assisted him in the field: 'Simon,     you
can't film it if you are not out there', and, 'You can only
be in one place at a time.'

These two simple phrases should be remembered by any would-be wildlife film-maker. The first demands that one's life is dedicated to the task of recording the world's wild things, leaving little room for anything else. By its very nature, most of what happens in the wild world is unpredictable. The only way to witness extraordinary events is always to be in a position that might allow you a privileged insight that few others will have. That means, quite simply, always being in the field. When you are tired, cold, wet and aching from head to toe with the effort of it all, you stay a little longer, watch a little harder, push yourself that little bit more. This is one way Hugh managed to achieve extraordinary results with the otters in Shetland when others before him had failed.

The second phrase – 'You can only be in one place at a time' – may sound like a platitude, but accepting the limitations of being alone in wild places is fundamental to remaining sane in pursuit of the elusive, rare and unpredictable events that become your Holy Grail. 'You should have been here yesterday', or words to that effect, is a phrase so often uttered by well-meaning people that it should be emblazoned across a T-shirt to be worn by all wildlife camera people. The gut-wrenching disappointment of being told that you should have been somewhere other than the place you were could cripple your essential sense of optimism. Only by steering by your own compass and deciding on the place to which you will commit your day's effort do you stand a chance of achieving sanguinity. You can be certain that a thousand extraordinary events are being played out every second of the day in many corners of the planet. You can also be certain that some of these events will be witnessed by people other than yourself, and that they, quite reasonably, will want to tell you about them. If you hop from one hunch to the next, influenced by what has just been seen, you will almost certainly be one step behind your whole life. If instead you have the courage of your convictions, based on sound knowledge and intuition, your time will come and you will be in the right place. Eventually.

It took me several more years to go to the right place. Not that the places I did visit were unpleasant, far from it. From the grass plains of Kenya to the South Atlantic seas, my career as a wildlife film-maker took me to some of the planet's most magnificent wilderness areas. On a more domestic scale, I worked on projects that demanded many months spent in stunningly beautiful corners of Britain. I made films on the west coast of Scotland about otters and red deer, and grew to know and love the ancient oak woods and ragged rocky coastline of that area. Whenever the option of basing myself in Shetland presented itself, I somehow found a reason why it was not suitable: the distance, the weather, the expense. Looking back, I believe the reasons behind my avoiding Shetland then were more personal and complex. On the one hand, there existed Hugh's definitive film and book on the otters there, and, perhaps misguidedly, I wanted to make my professional stamp from another part of the world. This was as much to do with a fear of comparison (in which I was certain I would come off worst) as it was a desire to discover new, filmable populations of otters in Britain. But more potently, I still did not want to meet the subject of my infatuation. I did not want to risk my idolised islands being a let-down.

From the moment I embarked on my career aged seventeen, appearing in front of a camera was as much a part of my professional life as was operating one. Presenting wildlife programmes for television has always been an exciting and fulfilling way of sharing my passion for the subject. This is never more true than with live broadcasts and, among those, the strands that have followed British wildlife across the seasons have been most enduring. *Springwatch*, in its various incarnations, is a series that has taken me to many of the wilder corners of the British Isles. To many, such as the spectacular seabird colonies of the Farne Islands off the east coast of northern England, to the Isle of Rum in the Inner Hebrides, I was a newcomer, having found a reasonable excuse at last to visit some of the nation's most renowned wildlife hot-spots. In the wake of the 2005 series, where I was based on the Farne Islands, near a peregrine nest in middle England and at the London Wetland Centre, I was asked by the series producers where I would like to visit next, with a view to spending the whole three weeks of transmission, and a week or so beforehand, filming in more or less one spot.

Where in the British Isles would I like to spend a month? Somewhere I had never been but about which I had obsessed. A place that I knew held a surprising variety of wild creatures, and the chance of some truly exceptional wild encounters. There was one destination that stood out above all others. At last I was going to meet the islands that had for so long been the subject of my dreams. I was going to Shetland.

# Chapter 2

## First Encounter

'Where's the airstrip?' I thought as the small propeller-powered aircraft banked and dropped towards the ocean. I had glimpsed land as we made the turn: great cliffs of jagged rock, topped by a whitewashed lighthouse, and then, through low clouds, small islands peppered the sea below, but still no sign of a conventional inland approach to a runway. I realised we were on our final approach and seemed to be heading for a narrow strip of land that tied the cliffy southern headland to the hills beyond. Carving the narrow causeway in two was the strip: its approach was the grey water of the sea; its overshoot the same. An aerial arrival in Shetland echoed what was to prove the theme of the land as a whole; it was a place dominated and influenced by the ocean at every turn.

Our pilot expertly brought his craft through the turbulent air on to terra firma and we taxied to the small terminal at Sumburgh Airport, the only public commercial airstrip on the isles. As the door opened, we were met by the other theme that was to run constant through most of our stay. Wind. Various folk ahead of me stooped to avoid bashing their scalps on the low doorframe and offered their heads to the Shetland breeze. For any who, like me, were follicly challenged, it was just the collar of their jacket that suggested any kind of buffeting, but for the more hirsute it was clear that this was no ordinary wind. Anyone who had started off with a good hair day soon received a thorough ruffling from the elements, so that by the time they reached the terminal building, it looked as though they had been given an electric shock. For the other newcomers and myself, the effect was like a slap in the face, but I welcomed it. I knew that the islands had a reputation for wind, even through the summer. Indeed, the Shetland community had been the butt of various jokes that suggested the moment the wind stopped blowing, the whole human population of the islands fell over, so used were they to leaning against the force of the gale. But for me the wild weather carried the scent of the sea, the promise of wild places and the spectacle of seabirds like gannets, puffins and fulmars holding their station in the air above their colonies.

By the time I reached the terminal building, a walk of a hundred metres or so from the plane, my luggage had already beaten me to the carousel; an all-time first in my years of flying the globe. I gratefully loaded my cases on to a trolley and wheeled them out to meet the rental car company representative.

'Will du be taken the car for wan wik or twa?' I was asked by the charming lady who met me with the keys.

'Two weeks at least, please,' I answered rather too eagerly. I felt that my first contact with the Shetland dialect had gone quite well, my ear well used to a Scottish brogue from my mother's Glaswegian origin and my time spent on the west coast of the Scottish mainland. I little realised that the kind lady was adapting her usual speech by what is known in Shetland as 'knapping', with a pronounced 'k' using an affected version of the local tongue that allows the untrained southern ear to penetrate what is otherwise an entirely new language. I would quickly discover that, in full flow, a conversation held in dialect would demand serious concentration on my part, and some careful study of the vocabulary. I would also discover that each island and region of the Shetland Isles hosts its own unique brand of dialect, so that a resident local of, say, the island of Whalsay might be little understood by a resident of Lerwick, and vice versa.

I had been exposed to some of the local words already, picking up a few of the Shetland terms for wild creatures through my reading and conversations with birdwatchers. One or two of these names were adopted more broadly by the British birdwatching community, the most famous perhaps being 'bonxie', the Shetland name for a great skua. What I did not realise until I started chatting with Shetlanders, however, is that 'bonxie', or 'bonksi', means something or someone who is thickset or dumpy, which, given the powerful physique of this avian raider, is very appropriate. Another Shetland name that had migrated south was tystie, the name given to the black guillemot, which found its origins in the Old Norse word *teisti*, referring to the bird's high, whistling call. I was to discover over time that many of the Shetland names for creatures were wonderfully descriptive and many had their roots firmly set in ancient Norse.

With my gear packed in the hire car, I headed north to

join the rest of the film crew at our hotel base, midway up the mainland. Despite having studied maps of the islands and asked about drive times, it still came as something of a shock to discover just how big the mainland of Shetland was. Thirty minutes after leaving the airport in the south I was only just reaching the main town of Lerwick. Along the way, it took all my self-control not to stop the car every few hundred metres to gaze at the view afforded by the winding main road. I flicked longing glances at the island of Mousa lying tantalisingly off the eastern coast. I was aching to pause and gaze across the bay at Cunningsburgh with its litter of rocky skerries that were hauling points for seals, but kept telling myself that there would be plenty of opportunity to explore and that I had to make it to the hotel in time for a scheduled production meeting.

A further forty minutes of driving on some of the best-maintained roads I had ever experienced in Britain found me entering the village of Brae and turning down a driveway to Busta House Hotel, where I and several members of the crew would be based for most of our stay.

Busta House overlooks a voe, a protected bay a little like a mini-fjord, on the threshold of Muckle Roe, a bulbous peninsula that pushes into Saint Magnus Bay and the Atlantic on the west of the mainland. Despite this being one of the more densely populated parts of the isles, it, like all of Shetland, has an air of being dominated by the sea and natural forces. In the comfort of the long living room, with the scent of peat burning in the open fire, I greeted other crew members and launched into conversations about our hopes and aspirations for the forthcoming few weeks of live broadcasts. I did my level best to concentrate fully, but could not help my thoughts wandering out through the window, down to the coast and the world of wild otters and shorebirds. I was trying to be grown-up about the professional task ahead, but the child in me wanted to run down to the tide-line and clamber over the rocks.

After an hour or so, and with a broad game plan in place, we went through to the restaurant, where we were joined by some of the people who had agreed to help us with our mission to reveal some of Shetland's rich fauna through the series. Among them, a couple of gentlemen with whom I could identify fully. John Campbell and Terry Holmes, both Englishmen from different walks of life, had come to Shetland almost twenty years earlier with a shared passion: otters. Both had coincidentally developed an otter addiction having been inspired by Hugh Miles's film, both had come to Shetland on holiday to try and watch the object of their infatuation, and both had ended up living on the isles.

When John first came to stay with his wife, Helen, they rented a variety of houses from which John could venture out otter-watching. Once, the daughter of one of the house-owners offered John a lift to the local shop and struck up a conversation to try and discover more about this gentle, rather secretive man.

'So, what brings you to Shetland?' she asked politely. What she thought she heard in response was John very candidly admitting he was an alcoholic.

'Oh, I see. Well, I guess you can get away from all that here,' she answered a little awkwardly.

'Oh no, I don't want to get away from it; this is where I can really indulge it!' said John enthusiastically.

'Ummm. Well, yes, I suppose you can,' the girl responded, now distinctly awkward. Seeing her discomfort, John asked the girl what she had thought he had said.

'Well, you told me you are an alcoholic, didn't you?'

John giggled and put her straight. 'Not an alcoholic – an otterholic!'

John and Terry had found each other through their shared passion and started a business taking holiday-makers out to see wild otters in Shetland. Knowing how tricky it can be to see an otter, let alone show others one, I asked them how on earth they managed to run a business of this nature, given the inevitable number of times their clients would be disappointed.

'Well, I'm not saying it can't happen, but we've not had a disappointed client so far.'

I was staggered. These men obviously knew their otters very well indeed, and I had the great good fortune to be working with them both for the next few weeks. The challenge of showing wild otters on live television was enormous, but if any two men were able to give us the chance of realising that goal, it was going to be John and Terry.

I was also introduced to an RSPB warden on Shetland who was to be key to our working with many of the bird species we hoped to film. Helen Moncrieff was a raven-haired lass with a ready smile and a mischievous sense of humour, born and raised on Shetland and one of those lucky people who was completely in love with the land of her origins. She was also hugely knowledgeable, not just about the bird life, but about the wildlife as a whole on the islands, and had an encyclopaedic knowledge of just about everyone and anyone who lived in Shetland. If we wanted to know about a man who had a boat, Helen would give us a list of ten who might be able to help. Diving? Helen had the answers. I have no doubt that if we had asked Helen where we might find a tightrope walker, she would have put us in touch with someone. She also had an intriguing and rather formidable reputation as a champion leg-wrestler, a talent I was to witness first hand or, to be more accurate, leg, later in my stay.

Before we got our teeth into otter-watching, or leg-wrestling, though, we wanted to visit a few of the islands' more remote locations to make short films that we could play in to the live shows over the coming weeks. To make one of these, we headed to the island of Noss off the east coast.

# Chapter 3

## Water Fairies and Dive Bombers

The island of Noss had been described by some of my bird-barmy friends as one of the ornithological wonders of Britain. Consequently, as we made the journey to the island with a view to completing a couple of short films ahead of the live programmes, I was armed with rich mental images: towering cliffs, the musky scent of seabird guano and the ringing call of kittiwakes echoing from the rock face, piercing through the sea surge hissing below. Unfortunately, my bubble of enthusiasm for the trip had been somewhat deflated by the onset of a bout of man-flu. It seems to be a seasonal tradition of mine – coming down with the lurgy just before a live transmission. On this occasion it might have had something to do with my just returning to the UK after months away in Africa, or simply mixing with a larger group of people than I was accustomed to. Whatever the cause, I was feeling pretty rough, with a throbbing headache, hot and cold flushes and aching joints as we arrived at the small jetty on the east side of the island of Bressay, awaiting the final leg of the journey, which would be made in a tiny inflatable boat courtesy of the wardens on the island reserve.

With kit and crew assembled after several shuttle runs across the narrow sound, we were at last in a position to make the final push on foot to the cliffs on the eastern seaboard of Noss. I normally relish a bit of physical exercise, some pulse-pumping to get the blood flowing. It makes the prize of reaching a magical place all the more delicious and satisfying. But on this occasion I looked at the mile or so of gentle ascent ahead of us with a degree of dread. By now I was sweating profusely and every muscle in my body was telling me to lie down and sleep. Not wanting to let the crew down and, frankly, still desperately keen to reach the seabird colonies for myself, I headed out with a lighter than usual load on my back.

Our guide across the island was Tim Sykes, warden on the reserve of several years' standing and a man who knew every inch of the near circular rocky isle. He kindly guided us off the public footpath that ran around the circumference of the island, so as not to disturb nesting birds, and instead struck out on a path right across the centre of the plateau that sweeps down from the high ground to the western shore. The reason this route is not normally encouraged is that it takes walkers through the heart of a bonxie colony. I've mentioned before that bonxies, or great skuas, are thickset birds; they look like gulls on steroids after a bout of mud wrestling. Their unassuming plumage, dark, chocolate-brown eyes and not particularly large bill belies a strength of body and character that have earned them both respect and a degree of revilement amongst many Shetlanders. I had seen innumerable still photographs of bonxies, many of which struck a familiar pose: wings outstretched, beak wide open, legs dangling; all taken on a wide-angle lens. In these photos the birds were clearly attacking the photographers. I knew they had a reputation for defending their nests and young against all comers, and I was about to discover that it was well earned.

With our guide ensuring we were well clear of any nests, we picked a winding route up the western slope of Noss; despite our care, there were one or two pugnacious skuas that decided to let us know who was boss in the neighbourhood. In my befuddled state, I didn't see the first attack until the bird was a few metres away, coming directly at my face at head level with an intensity of gaze that suggested it had the guts and the guile to see through its onslaught. I instinctively flinched and ducked as the bonxie spread his wings, opened his beak and let out a screech like a banshee's just a metre or so from my face. He bounced into the air above my head, twisted on a wing tip and came back for another pass, in a near vertical stoop, at the top of my head.

'Don't worry, Simon, he probably won't hit you,' came the almost encouraging words from Tim. It was the 'probably' bit that disturbed me. I have been hit in the head by herring gulls, lesser black-backed gulls, white-chinned petrels, prions and South Atlantic skuas. The latter being southern cousins of the bonxies, they would pack, I assumed, a very similar punch. I didn't particularly relish the idea of adding great skua to the list of birds that had already beaten me on points, with the occasional knockout to their credit.

I need not have been concerned. After a few alarming bluffs, the bird that had taken such a dislike to me landed next to his mate some fifty metres away, threw his wings back in a heraldic pose, thrust his head forward and, I could have sworn, laughed uproariously. He was, of course, displaying to his mate, letting her know what a top bloke he was and how marvellous he had been at scaring the funny man in the bobble hat. The call was very much a part of a ritual that skuas indulge when defending their nest sites against competitors of the same species, or when one or other bird has been away for a while and rejoins its mate. Or maybe he really was just having a giggle.

The rest of the hike passed without incident bar the increased level of exhaustion I was suffering as a result of my raging temperature. The final push to the summit – OK, the last few hundred metres up the gentle slope to the eastern cliffs – had me gasping for breath, but once there my breath was short for an entirely different reason. Before me was a natural amphitheatre of epic grandeur. One hundred and eighty-metre cliffs swept in a half bowl down to the surge of a gentle swell in the ocean below. I was immediately struck by the organic twists and swirls of the eroded sandstone that gave the impression that the whole cliff was made from melted wax. A quick glance through my binoculars revealed that virtually every crevice, ledge and stony hammock was occupied by one seabird or other. Guillemots shuffled for space on ledges no bigger than their awkward feet would allow. Razorbills nestled in pairs in more discreet alcoves, and fulmars cackled and swung their heads to and fro in declarations of love. Kittiwakes startled the natural palette of black, with their grey and white plumage and blood-red gapes, uttering their name in piercing sibilance, but it was the gannets that stole the show. Eight thousand pairs graced this seabird tenement block. Sixteen thousand examples of the nation's biggest seabird and, in my opinion, among the most impressive and beautiful birds in the world, added their guttural calls to the cacophony below. Even in my feverish state, I was blown away by the astonishing natural spectacle before me.

Over the ensuing couple of hours I coughed and spluttered my way through some pieces to camera, trying to convey how genuinely thrilled I was to be here, despite my bloodshot eyes and shivering body. I knew I would have to leave Noss before truly enjoying it as I should, but I made a vow then that I would return to the cliffs again someday, hopefully in rather better health, to explore them more fully.

After a night back in the hotel, dosed up to the hilt with my favourite flu remedy – a very stiff hot toddy – I was in much better form to continue my exploration of the isles over the following days. On our filming wish list was a small bird with a big personality. Red-necked phalaropes are rare in the UK: only about 40 pairs breed annually, and the majority of those do so in the Shetland Islands. It wasn't simply their scarcity, but also their rather liberated breeding behaviour that tickled our interest.

I travelled with the crew to Fetlar, one of the northerly isles in the archipelago, to meet the man who had dedicated a large chunk of his life to the protection and understanding of these charming little birds. Malcolm Smith, or Malcie, as he was known to all, was a warden for the RSPB on the islands of Fetlar, Yell and Unst. We met at his house for a prebrief about the birds, and his calm manner, rugged good looks and deep voice, coloured by the lilt of an accent from the Isle of Lewis, gave him the air of a quietly confident man very much on top of his game. As we pored over maps, sipping mugs of strong tea in his kitchen that overlooked a magnificent bay bordered by cliffs, a bubble of excitement rose in my chest. I was still an RNP virgin (RNP is the birder's abbreviation for red-necked phalarope), but almost felt I had seen them before, so vivid were the images of these diminutive little wading birds in my mind's eye. I had gazed at innumerable photographs and studied illustrations of them for years, marvelling at their delicate structure and designer plumage. But it was their curious breeding behaviour that really captured my imagination. Most bird species share parental duties or, if only one of the pair is left to raise the kids, it's the female. This is where the phalarope differs. Each spring the birds arrive from a winter spent on the oceans of the tropics and immediately set about courting. But rather than a gang of males strutting their stuff, it is the females that don the dandy plumage and try to win the hearts of the male birds which, in their drab grey and brown summer dress, are very hard to please.

Malcie talked us through the likely scenario we would witness once we reached one of the breeding locations of the birds he was monitoring, and then we set off to the secret pools a few miles from his house.

I spotted the phalaropes the moment we crested a low

hill that overlooked a tiny loch perched in picturesque fashion close to some sea cliffs. Among the rushes, which were leaning against their undisturbed mirror image on this windless day, dashed the silhouetted forms of a couple of fragile-looking birds with long, stick-thin beaks. They darted restlessly, stabbing at the surface of the pool, as though attacking their own reflections rather than snatching any food items. They were tiny, smaller than I had imagined, and because of the light conditions I could see nothing of their colouring, so couldn't tell if they were males or females.

We carefully approached the loch and moved into a position that allowed us to scan the pool with the sun behind us. I momentarily lost track of the phalaropes I had seen from the crest, until I realised that I was searching too far into the centre of the pool; for there, in front of me, and no further than ten metres away, was one of them swirling and pirouetting close to the shore. Its bold white stripe of the eye, charcoal grey head and blaze of russet down the neck revealed that it was a female in her breeding finery. And what a gorgeous vision she was.

I moved slowly down to the shoreline and was thrilled and surprised by the phalarope's lack of fear. She continued her frenetic path towards the spot where I was now crouching on the shore, and only when she was about a metre away did she lift her head and paddle away a short distance before resuming her feeding. I could clearly see the tiny flies she was snatching for on the surface of the loch, and reflected on the vast number of these tiny snacks it would take to satisfy her, despite her diminutive frame.

Suddenly Malcie hissed in excitement, 'Look Simon, there's one coming in now! I'll bet it's just arrived from its migration. If it's a male, we'll see some fireworks!'

I looked up to see another phalarope, pin-legs dangling and wings arched in a bow as it cruised down to the loch. Around me a high-pitched twittering lifted out of the reeds and I was suddenly aware of at least three individual birds swimming rapidly into open water to greet the new arrival. The traveller settled on the loch about twenty metres away, but not for long. A mottled head and breast revealed that it was indeed a male, and the presence of this new bird on the block was clearly overwhelming for the girls. The three females already in residence on the pool fluttered rapidly across the water's surface and almost bumped into each other and the male in their enthusiastic dash to impress him. He, perhaps understandably after having made an epic journey over the open sea, looked a little weary and singularly unimpressed.

What followed was a charming, if somewhat comical and chaotic attempt on the part of each of the females to secure the male as their mate. Spinning, bumping, fluttering and calling in his face as he tried, often in vain, to get a bite to eat and a little peace.

He eventually, and without ceremony, followed one of the displaying girls to the shallows, where he leapt briefly on to her back and mated.

Job done!

Having made his choice he was now committing himself to a summer of single parenthood, for once the eggs were laid in the nest, secreted in a tussock of long grass close to the shore of the loch, the female would have nothing more to do with them. The male alone would incubate the brood and raise the chicks to the point of fledging and independence. The female would head back to the loch, perhaps to find another male to flirt and mate with; or perhaps simply to feed and rest before flying back out to sea, where once again she would dart and dip across the ocean's vast expanse.

As I sat on the loch border, I was joined by one of the female phalaropes, which paddled feverishly in the shallows and picked at bugs and flies on or near the surface of the pool. Now no more than a couple of metres away, I marvelled that such a tiny, fragile-looking bird could withstand a life on the open wave. Yet another wondrous facet of this charming, enigmatic bird.

Our time on Fetlar was fulfilling but limited, and soon we had to head back to the mainland, where preparations were in full flow for the imminent live transmissions.

After much deliberation, we had agreed to try to include views of otters in the first week of live broadcasting. We all knew that this would be a very big ask, given the elusive nature of the animals and the very brief periods during the hour-long transmissions that we would be on air. In each programme, our contribution amounted to about fifteen or twenty minutes of airtime, spread over the hour. Fifteen minutes during which we hoped we could show the viewing public of Britain live images of a ghost. Yeah, right!

# Chapter 4

## Otters, Oiks and Orcas

John Campbell and Terry Holmes had been dedicating hundreds of hours to finding the ideal location for our ambitious proposal. Both had favourite spots for otter-watching, but the location not only had to deliver animals reliably, but also match a host of technical and access requirements that narrowed the options down considerably.

In the end, a spot was decided upon that was away from the beaten track but still moderately accessible for all the heavy equipment necessary for the broadcasts. It also afforded a wide, panoramic view of a stretch of coastline along which John and Terry had watched otters for years. This summer had seen two females successfully rearing cubs within a few hundred metres of each other, and both territories were patrolled by the same large dog otter. There was the chance, then, that any one of six individual otters might pop out at any time, though I already knew their activity cycle would be far from random. Otters that use coastal waters tend to have preferences for certain sea conditions when it comes to finding a meal. Broadly speaking, they all tend to be busiest as the tide is dropping, or nearing its lowest point, or else on the rise shortly afterwards. There has been a lot of speculation and study

into the reasons why this should be. One obvious suggestion is that the less water the otter has to dive through to
reach the weedy bottom and the likely zone for foraging,
the easier the task will be for it. Perhaps the couple of
extra metres at high tide just add to the pressure – quite
literally – of staying under water long enough to find a
fish or a crab. It's likely too that, as the tide moves, so
fish tend to be busiest and therefore exposing themselves
to an otter on the prowl. But speculation can be futile:
there are always individual otters that buck convention
and hunt soon after dawn, or at dusk, regardless of tide
state. The otters that John and Terry hoped we would see
came from the 'tide-dependent' school of hunting, and as
such their likely activity periods slipped by about an hour
each day. This gave us a rough timetable from which to
work and to target our efforts at trying to reveal them on
live telly.

Before the broadcasts, though, we wanted to get some
views of the families 'in the bank' to illustrate what we
were looking for. Two first-class specialist cameramen were
deployed for the task: John Aitchison and Charlie
Hamilton-James. Both men were very familiar with
working with wild otters, having spent thousands of hours
following them for other projects. In addition to detailed
views of the otters, I also wanted to shoot a short film
showing a bit of field-craft; a 'how to' guide that would
feature a shot or two including both the animal and me
watching it.

I set off with Charlie on a rising tide to the location,
and waited on the high ground overlooking the bay. Charlie

had already spent time with John and Terry and had a good handle on the likely spots to search. Before long we glimpsed the telltale bobbing cork of an otter surfacing from a dive about thirty metres off shore.

'Let's wait for her to dive, then get down there,' I whispered unnecessarily to Charlie, who knew perfectly well how to approach an otter. Once she had gained her breath and dipped beneath the surface, we scrambled to our feet and trotted down to the shoreline. I had a tiny video camera to which I would speak once I had made my way alone to the foreshore; meanwhile Charlie lugged a full-size video kit with telephoto zoom lens. Our aim was to try to predict where the otter would come to the land, and line up a shot with me in the foreground, the otter in the background. For some ten minutes or so, she kept popping to the surface with small fish, and chewed them while treading water, unaware of our presence but staying too distant for Charlie to get the shots we were after. Having finished off five or six fish in this fashion, she made a long low dive and popped up much closer to us.

'Looks like she's coming in to have a sniff around,' whispered Charlie and, sure enough, she was making a beeline for the rocks to our right. We trotted, as fast as we were able, to get into position, knowing that once she made it on to land we would not be able to move for fear of being spotted. The wind was in our favour, blowing our scent away from the water, but the land behind us was low-lying, making it difficult for us to keep our silhouettes from breaking the horizon. We only just made it into position as the otter reached the first of the emergent rocks on the shore and walked on to the beach. I flung myself on to my side and kept my head low. I could not see her, but I could hear her sniffing not more than five or six metres away.

I slowly turned my head to see if Charlie had a clear view, and was happy to see his eye to the camera eyepiece, obviously following her movements. I dared to lift my head a little, moving as slowly as I was able, to try and pinpoint where the otter had walked. I had shifted just a few centimetres before I had to freeze. There she was, not more than a couple of metres from me, clambering over the rocks in my direction. This was not what I had planned. The last thing in the world I wanted to do was scare her, but if she kept on this path she would bump straight into me. As she came closer still, she hesitated, perhaps catching a faint whiff of human scent, or seeing a strange blob on this beach she knew so well. Her neck craned higher and she moved her head from one side to the other, trying to get a fix on the foreign object that was me. Thankfully, rather than run off in fear, she decided a gentle discretionary retreat would suffice and walked away a metre or so before lifting her tail and letting me know in no uncertain terms who was the rightful steward of the beach. I could clearly smell the scent of her fresh spraint – one I liken to sweet straw or musky violets and not at all unpleasant.

Our encounter was brief but, for me, thrilling. Truly close contact with an otter in Shetland and another seal on my fate as a hopeless otter junkie. The sequence of my lying in the seaweed next to a wild otter gave the live programmes a real taste of what makes these creatures so charismatic, even though – as we had predicted – it proved very difficult to show the viewing public live images of them. Despite all the hard work and precise observations, when we finally started transmitting live on weekday evenings, it became even more apparent that we would be very lucky indeed to realise our goal. We had otters swimming before our cameras minutes before we were on air, and others bringing fish to shore when other elements of the live programme were playing out from the base in Devon, hosted by Bill Oddie and Kate Humble, only to disappear when the cameras cut back to Shetland. At the end of the third show I apologised to the nation for not having brought them a live image of an otter. And then at last it happened.

On the fourth evening, all the stars lined up, the tide was at an ideal height, the rain and low cloud had paused, the gales had relented, and a couple of otters, a female we had named Flow, and her well-grown cub, had just started fishing as we went on air. Unfortunately they were swimming away from our main camera positions, and with all the technical trappings of the live transmission, John Aitchison was not able to follow them on foot. But he did keep a careful eye on them with the help of John Campbell and Terry spotting from the high ground. And at last, we had live pictures of wild otters on *Springwatch*. A first for television. OK, they were a long way off and you had to screw your eyes up to see them: brown animals, barely moving on brown rocks covered with brown seaweed; but they were definitely there. Just.

We featured a great deal besides otters on the shows, of course, from puffins and red-throated divers to fulmars and storm petrels. But one of the stars proved to be a bird that is widespread over much of coastal Britain, the oyster-catcher. 'Oiks', as they are fondly known by birdy folk, or 'shalder' in Shetland dialect, are familiar birds of the seashore, their bold pied plumage and piping calls making them about as subtle as a brick. I have to confess to wondering if we should be showcasing a bird that was not a regional speciality of the isles, but after chatting to a few Shetlanders I soon realised that they play an important part in the cultural calendar there.

Most, if not all, of the Shetland oystercatchers leave the isles in the late autumn, heading south, usually to feed along the English shores of the Irish Sea. The consequence of this itinerant lifestyle is that they are fondly received as a harbinger of spring when they return to their northerly breeding grounds from late February onwards. Oiks are everywhere on the isles, nesting in shallow scrapes wherever the ground allows, from heather moor to shingle beach. With natural real estate at a premium, some are forced – or perhaps choose – to raise a family in less conventional settings. We found nests in the top of rotting fence posts, on gravel drives leading up to houses, and one in a lay-by close to one of the busiest roads on the mainland (though the description 'busy' is of course relative. Even at rush hour, you would hardly describe Shetland as suffering from congestion.)

The nest we decided to feature was on a patch of grazed meadow, close to a single-track road in the northeast of the mainland. The location was unremarkable in many ways, but was subject to regular traffic in the form of free-ranging sheep. This, we thought, would inevitably lead to a degree of conflict, and as such would offer an engaging story for us to follow through the programme transmission period of three weeks. The hunch paid off, since there were many moments when we thought the whole clutch would be smashed as a frolicking mob of lambs, preoccupied by their games of chase and king of the castle, careered in the direction of the nest. Their saviour came in the form of two irate parent oystercatchers, piping wildly and flying directly at the faces of the oncoming lambs. Once or twice, a lamb would appear that was driven to greater curiosity by the fluttering forms of the adult oystercatchers, and would make the mistake of walking closer still to the nest scrape. This is when mum and dad unleashed their final weapon, landing on the head of the offending trespasser and pecking it hard between the eyes. When you consider that these same beaks are designed to lift limpets away from rocks and prise open mussels, you will appreciate that the effect of a direct hit is shocking, to say the least.

The whole clutch of four eggs hatched successfully and, despite a tense few days when the tiny chicks looked as though they were auditioning for a stage show of the 1980s hit TV series *Fame*, with their legs tangled in wool moulted from the local sheep flock, they all managed to scuttle through the earliest dangers that life threw at them.

If our oystercatcher soap opera offered some subtle

charm with a common bird, high drama was to come in the form of creatures that were much scarcer: the biggest predators to patrol our shores. We had heard that, from time to time, orcas, or killer whales, paid the coastline a visit. I knew that pods of these dynamic, ocean-going hunters had been seen around some of the Western Isles of Scotland in the past, but Shetlanders had reported increasingly frequent sightings in recent years, all around the archipelago. Despite the potential, we knew our chances of being in the right place at the right time to see them were very slim indeed.

Orcas, as I prefer to call them, since it defuses the rather sensational notion that they are dangerous and murderous (which is unjust, unless you are a herring or a seal), tend to keep on the move, pausing briefly to hunt seals or shoals of fish on their marine peregrinations. Capturing live views during a transmission might never happen even if we dedicated hundreds of years to the task, but having the chance to record some images of them would add a thrilling element of charismatic megafauna to the mix. Our first excitement came with a phone call from an enthusiastic local naturalist who had spotted a pod of orcas killing a seal off one of the most dramatic stretches of coastline in Shetland. Eshaness is in the northwest of the mainland and presents a barrier of precipitous cliffs to the ravages of the North Atlantic. A great stone arch known as Dore Holm sits about a kilometre off shore, and is perfectly placed at certain times of the year for viewing spectacular sunsets, which nestle on the ocean's surface framed by its natural gateway.

We arrived at the cliffs some forty-five minutes after the call, but already it was too late. A small group of observers was still present and, though well meaning, added a little salt to the wound of our having arrived too late by recounting the astonishing events that had passed twenty minutes earlier. The orcas had, apparently, caught a grey seal just off shore. They had then proceeded to play with it, a macabre game that included flicking it into the air with their powerful tail flukes. I could well imagine the scene, having had the good fortune to watch and film orcas in Argentina. There, the orcas had played with sea-lion pups for forty minutes or more before devouring them, on one notable occasion throwing the carcass well over twenty metres skywards. Just why they have a tendency to do this no one really knows. It could be to flay the flesh from the bones, or perhaps it is a way of practising a killer blow with their tails. Whatever the reason, I knew we had missed something very special, and was resigned to the fact that I had still never seen orcas in British waters. Knowing that they were cruising the shores certainly added an air of expectancy to each day, though, and a frisson of excitement to every phone call that came in from the network of self-appointed orca watchers on the islands.

Days had passed since the Eshaness sighting when, on the morning of the weekend before we were finishing the series, we received news that a pod had been seen moving fast along the shores on the west side of the mainland. Cameraman John Aitchison was scrambled to the location and I followed soon afterwards. By the time I reached

Trondra, the island where the last reported sighting had been made, a period of at least half an hour had passed, time enough for the orcas to have moved many kilometres along the shoreline or to have disappeared altogether out to sea. I stopped my car in a passing place on the single-track road and scanned the waters of the channel that was bordered by East Burra and West Burra. When you look for a creature this dynamic and unpredictable, it's always difficult to imagine you will ever see it. The sea looks too big, the waves too high to stand a chance of picking out the ephemeral flash of a creature from the depths breaking surface to snatch a breath. And so it was that my first glimpse felt unreal. Off in the distance, in the narrow sound, a flash of black, followed by another. I knew what I had seen but still needed to hold my excitement in check before I could categorically confirm the owners of the fins. And then there was my proof. As I studied the grey waters with binoculars where my naked eye had spied what I took to be the dorsal fins of female orcas, the surface broke with the tip of another. This time, though, the fin grew and grew until it rose up above the surface, well over a metre, cutting a black delta against the grey of the sea. A bull orca . . . 'A BULL ORCA!'

I heard myself saying the words, trying to ensure that the vision became real through being articulated. No doubt about it, no possible confusion with a porpoise or even one of the more infrequent Risso's dolphins that can get you in a muddle at a distance. There is nothing else on earth that looks like this. To describe a bull orca's fin will do the vision a disservice, but I'll have a stab at it anyway.

It is like the energy of the restless sea, like the essence of all that is magical about a surprise encounter in the natural world. There it was, surging forward with a stream of spray breaking across its leading edge, betraying the great speed and power of the creature beneath.

A garbled shout of exhilaration burst from my lips as I dashed back to the car and drove on, trying to get ahead of the orcas' progress and so make it down to the shore before they passed by. I pulled in to a gateway about a kilometre further on, and a quick scan with binoculars revealed John Aitchison, camera in position, standing on a headland overlooking the sound. He too had been tracking the fast-moving pod and was primed for their next pass.

I ran as fast as I was able across a couple of fields to the shoreline and joined John.

I reached his side and, with my hands on my thighs, half bent with a stitch and gasping for breath, I asked if he had seen them.

'They're moving like the clappers, Si. I just get a few short glimpses and the next time I see them they're a kilo-metre away.'

'They should be coming through here any second; I saw them heading this way just now,' I added, and joined John's vigil, scanning the choppy waters of Grunasound. There was a long five minutes of nothing, with an increasing feeling of hollow disappointment coming in waves. Had the pod passed us by under water? They were most certainly capable of doing so. Pangs of self-doubt washed over me, and the split desires to hold my ground and at the same time run back to the car and check the coast-line further south wrestled for priority. Just as I was about to suggest I make a dash for it and phone John if I came across them, they arrived. One hundred metres or so from shore, the sickle-shaped fins of two female orcas broke the surface. They were followed by two, then three more: great black knives slicing the waters in two. But they gave way to a giant as the bull, now much closer and all the more impressive, rolled into view, took a breath and cruised on. His fin seemed to take an age to disappear, the last vestige of the tip slipping beneath the waves with a theatrical spray and splash.

I glanced across at John who was concentrating on recording the passage of the giants before he looked briefly across at me with a broad grin. It still took some believing: at least six orcas cruising the shores of Britain, on a mission – it seemed – to find a meal, quite probably hunting some of the common seals that were giving birth at this time of year. For just a moment their world and ours was joined by their mammalian dependence on air and our insatiable desire to connect with the wild spirits of the earth. My veins pulsed with a mixture of adrenalin and the effort of running across to the shoreline. My face ached with a smile. They next surfaced a good five hundred metres further south, almost out of view and dwarfed by the sea again. But in my mind's eye they remained huge, an imposing presence that would forever colour my view of the shoreline here.

That was the best view I had of the orcas during my first visit to Shetland in 2006. We managed to film them again, quite probably a different group, chasing around the RSPB reserve of Sumburgh Head, the most southerly reach of the mainland, but my personal relationship with these wolves of the sea was tantalisingly brief. I knew I would return to try and connect with them again. Shetland had bitten deeper into my psyche than I could have imagined even in my boyhood dreams, and not just because of the wildlife. The people, too, had touched me in a way that very few other communities have done.

It is tricky and potentially patronising to try and encapsulate the essence of a people. A community is, of course, by its very definition, as disparate and varied as the souls it harbours. Perhaps it was the people with whom I connected, those who had a love for the natural world and the rhythm of the land, that coloured my view of Shetlanders, but there were common traits that ran through their convivial manner. Perhaps the most prevalent was a sense of unaffected pride and confidence. They knew they were born into a place that had a unique charm, and one that was not overt or crass. To love Shetland was to embrace its hard edges, its storms and dark winters, its treeless skyline and howling gales, because in that embrace came precious access to wildness, beauty, peace, space and, perhaps most importantly of all, a sense of freedom. Only when you have spent time in a place that allows endless walks over hills and valleys, along rugged coastline and white-sand beaches, and known that you are alone with your thoughts and your own pulse, can you begin to feel a hint of that freedom. Simply being born into Shetland life was, I knew, no guarantee that you would be bewitched by it. Many spoke of relatives or friends who had headed south at the first opportunity and never returned. But if you found it in yourself to love the contrasts, however extreme, of this wild land, you would find a peace and sense of belonging that is all too rare in our crowded lives.

I experienced this confidence and warmth many times in my brief stay in 2006. Whether it was in the bars of Lerwick, where I was approached – with a cordiality that bore no hint of sycophancy – for a chat about my work and life, and in turn enjoyed discovering all about theirs, or through working alongside the charismatic wonder that is Helen Moncrieff. Helen's world was driven by the smiles that the pupping of the seals inspired in her, or the arrival of the terns in spring. She spoke with animated joy of the storm petrels that nested in Mousa Broch, and she crooned to the puffins that waddled with comical pomp across the grassy headlands. Her home was her love, and I was jealous of her clear sense of identity and affinity with the place. And if that were not enough, she held the RSPB's leg-wrestling title.

I had vaguely heard of the homespun sport, more usually conducted by rugby players in bars after a game than female wardens of nature reserves, and was intrigued by her claim. I was to discover just how formidable she was at the art when I accepted her challenge to a leg-wrestling match after a drink or two towards the end of our shooting the *Springwatch* series. A couple of the other crew members, both strapping lads, were before me in line for the challenge. Each of them was hurled on to their sides with no more than what appeared to be a flick of the knee on Helen's part. And then it was my turn.

'Just lie there, next to me, head to toe,' instructed Helen. I lay close to her right side, shoes off, hoping that my socks were not too smelly.

'That's it, now, right leg up, and wrapped around mine,' she declared.

I did as I was told and was now in a comical embrace, thigh to thigh, the back of our knees each wrapped around the other.

'I did my back in recently so I'm suposed to be in retirement,' Helen said. 'The doctor said I shouldn't do this any more.'

'How did you injure your back?' I asked, concerned.

'Beating half the reserve staff in one night. Ready . . . ? On my count of three. ONE, TWO . . .'

I didn't have time to protest. I braced myself against the floor with the palms of my hands and took the strain with my leg. I'd go gently, I thought. The last thing I wanted to do was to injure Helen any further.

'. . . THREE!'

The next thing I knew I seemed to be flying in a twisting arc over Helen and into a crumpled heap with my face on the floor on her left side, staring at her feet. I didn't know what had hit me! I wasn't just beaten: I was thrashed. I'd like to say that I didn't really put up a fight; that I was careful not to put too much into the contest for fear of exacerbating Helen's injury, but the truth is that I gave it everything I had and was utterly and completely outclassed.

With typical humility, Helen stood and helped me to my feet.

'Well done, Simon, good try.'

I'd be back for a rematch one of these days.

# Chapter 5

## Shetland Revisited

My professional and personal lives are inescapably joined at the hip. In fact, a more accurate analogy would be to say that they are Siamese twins with shared vital organs. Neither can exist without the other, yet both can, at times, be at loggerheads. Wildlife film-making is a time-consuming, all-absorbing commitment, not a job. There is no nine to five. No one counts the hours worked, because it would be the same as counting the hours lived. As such, the vocation can take its toll and some elements of life can suffer from neglect. Family life is one. The passions that fuel and drive my professional sincerity have, in the past, scarred others. My three older children from my first marriage, Alexander, Romy and Greer, now all mature or maturing into wonderful independent souls, saw little of me when they were young. I suffered too from my long absences and missing the precious moments of their journey through life.

My young daughter from my second marriage, Savannah, has had a rather different exposure to my world. My wife, Marguerite, is a wildlife film-maker too. She shares the passions, the commitment and the dogged perseverance needed to achieve candid views of rare and ephemeral moments. When we decided to start a family together, it was with the clear understanding that we would do everything in our power to avoid either one of us becoming a film-maker's 'widow'. We shared a passion for the natural world, for each other, and for the prospect of introducing our daughter to the rich lives we lead, rather than having one or other of us stay at home while the other travelled and worked. As a result, Savannah has travelled with us to Kenya on several occasions, and is as much at home eating her lunch alongside a pride of lions as she is walking in the green fields of Britain. When contemplating projects, Marguerite and I try to ensure that they are sympathetic to our being together most – if not all – of the time. This rule shrinks our planet a little. Camping in hard polar environments is off limits until Savannah's fingers are robust enough not to snap off in temperatures of -30°C. Living under the stars in deserts may have to wait a year or two. Shetland, on the other hand, is perfect. It combines the contradictions of being at once remote and accessible, its weather can be extreme but rarely life threatening, and it offers access to wilderness with easy human comforts. The perfect place for life, little people and work to meld.

After returning to England in the wake of my visit to Shetland in 2006, I almost immediately started hatching plans to return. Marguerite had visited the islands when we were shooting *Springwatch* and had accompanied me to the hills overlooking bays where otters foraged, despite being seven months pregnant with Savannah. She too had been smitten with the sense of freedom and wilderness that seeped through the peat and hung in the wind, and agreed that it would be a great place to work for a couple of years.

My original proposition to the BBC Natural History Unit was to make a one-hour film that followed a family of otters, whilst also featuring my own family, in a remote corner of Shetland. The series editor of the *Natural World* strand was sympathetic to the idea and provided some development funding to allow me to make a short trip to the isles to search for suitable accommodation and locations.

It was February 2008 by the time I had pulled together the necessary flights, contacts and itinerary to make the trip north. I was to be accompanied by my friend and colleague Charlie Hamilton-James. Charlie too had a passion for Shetland, one that had matured beyond my own over the years. As a teenager he had begged his mother to take him there to watch otters (also having been inspired by Hugh Miles's book and film) and was given a baptism of fire, being dropped off at a remote ferry port and given the freedom to find his own way. Despite foul weather and elusive quarry, Charlie found the pervasive, intoxicating undercurrent of Shetland seep into his bones and never looked back, spending summer holidays and winters there, and driving through the night to help rescue oiled seabirds, seals and otters during the MV *Braer* oil tanker disaster in 1993. His network of friends, his knowledge of the islands' topography and his obsession with otters would all be invaluable assets during our brief reconnoitre.

We arrived in Shetland on the short but unreasonably expensive flight from Bristol via Glasgow to a near perfectly still day. Both Charlie and I knew how rare this was. In the Shetland dialect, these conditions are known fondly as 'days atween wadders' or days between weathers, suggesting, quite reasonably, that it wouldn't last long. A still, bright, late winter day offers the very best conditions for otter-watching. Most of the otters in Shetland feed almost exclusively in the sea, and spotting one against choppy water can be a real challenge. By contrast, if the sea's surface is like a millpond, as it was on our arrival, you can pick out the low profile of a swimming otter at a great distance. In addition, the ripples caused by their diving or the delta 'V' of their bow-wake as they swim on the surface catches the light and points to their whereabouts. *Ring of Bright Water*, the title of the classic book by Gavin Maxwell, which tells the story of a couple of otters he kept as pets on the Isle of Skye, sums up the animal's effect on a still loch or surface of the sea.

Otters are also creatures of comfort, despite dipping regularly into waters that might be no more than 7°C through the winter. If the weather above the surface is harsh or inclement, they spend only the time they must out fishing and then run back to the warmth and comfort of their underground holts, once the job of getting a meal is done. If the air is still and the sun is shining, they are much more inclined to relax on the rocks and seaweed between bouts of fishing, rolling to dry their coats and falling into long, deep slumbers before the rising tide or a rumbling tummy stirs them once more.

'I know we should be looking for houses, but what about a quick scout for otters first?' I suggested to Charlie, knowing full well that, as a fellow otter junkie, he would readily agree to the plan.

We drove slowly north from Sumburgh, me at the wheel,

Charlie scouring the waters of the east coast for a glimpse of the telltale black 'cork' of an otter, popping to the surface after a dive. Before long he had his first sighting.

'Got one, about fifty metres offshore . . . Pull in just here,' Charlie urged, and I swung the rented car into a lay-by. We had only been travelling for twenty minutes or so, and already our first otter of the trip was under our belts. We both left the car and watched the otter fishing casually across the bay, before I looked at my watch.

'Better get to the hotel and check in. I think we'll see one or two more before we have to go.' I reluctantly pulled myself away from the beautiful vista, the bay reflecting the amber hills and marked by the silver ripples made by the otter, and, with Charlie, drove on to Busta House Hotel near Brae.

Charlie made a series of phone calls to friends around the isles, and that evening we planned an itinerary for the next few days. We would see as much of Shetland as we could, checking houses that Charlie knew from his time here and visiting others that we had been tipped off about by friends. Once again, Helen Moncrieff had been an unflinching ally, calling around her friends and relatives to find out if they had houses for rent that might suit our purpose. I was hoping to find somewhere that was isolated (but not dangerously so, since we intended to return with my baby daughter Savannah); close to the sea, and with the promise of lots of great wildlife on the doorstep, especially otters.

Contrary to our expectations, the weather held fair for most of our short stay, giving us ample opportunity to explore stretches of coastline that Charlie had identified as being 'hot' for otters during his years on Shetland, and also to visit a number of houses he had either stayed in or else thought might be suitable for the project I had in mind. We also contacted and met up with a number of people who we either both knew or were friends of Charlie. One such couple was Bo and Henry Anderton from the west of the mainland. Charlie had worked for Henry when he was living on Shetland, helping out with a hotel they ran at the time, and living part time in their house. Henry was the laird of a large tract of ground west of the village of Walls, but the title did not grant him great wealth or privilege. Instead, he was a softly spoken, charming and very hard-working man who now, with his wife Bo, ran a small delicatessen and restaurant in Lerwick called the Olive Tree. I was introduced to them after Charlie and I had been walking a few miles of coastline, looking at houses in various states of ruin and spotting the odd otter, and was greeted by a warm kitchen, a mug of tea and the offer of some toast.

'Where did the bread come from?' I asked, salivating at the sight of a warm, crusty, seeded loaf being cleaved into generous slices to be toasted under the grill.

'I make it,' answered Bo with a glow of unassuming pride. 'Here you go.' She passed me a couple of slices of toast on a plate and gestured to the pot of butter on the kitchen table. 'Help yourself. There's Marmite or jam, whichever you wish.'

There are few foods more comforting than hot buttered toast. But this was 'sublime-melt-in-your-mouth-malty-delicious-drizzled-with-melting-butter-and-lashings-of-

Close encounters with a puffin.

There are over 100 islands in the Shetland archipelago.
Noss from the air.

The reality of Shetland exceeds expectations. Eshaness in 2006.

Puffins nest in colonies dotted around the islands. One of the finest is on the RSPB reserve at Sumburgh Head.

One of the most endearing features of otters is their sense of fun. The mother and large male cub we followed in the summer of 2008, playing in the surf.

The freedom to run feral. Savannah in an iris jungle.

Who needs a TV when you've got a beach? Nick Jordan filming
Savannah and me looking for crabs.

Our idyllic house on the hill, before the weather changed.

Access to the house was via a beautiful beach. Easy in the summer, not so straightforward in winter.

That's how it should be done! Summer sheep shearing.

Savannah's first Viking. Lerwick.

The inimitable Helen Moncrieff, RSPB Warden and all round wonderful person, checking puffin burrows.

Our local, the Pierhead at Voe. Top pint, top chips.

Killer whales sometimes come remarkably close to shore, hunting seals.

Nothing can prepare you for the sheer scale, charisma and beauty of
a killer whale travelling at top speed.

Marmite-toast'. This was the king of all toasts. I immediately fell in love with Bo. Marguerite would understand.
I hoped Henry would too.

We chatted about otters and houses and I was sucked
into the warmth of the house and the company, but eventually, reluctantly, had to prise myself away from the kitchen
table and make a move. We still had a few more locations
to check before darkness fell and, with little more than
six hours of daylight, we were running short of time. We
thanked Bo and Henry and bade them farewell at the
door, the last vestigial scent of warm toast clinging to my
clothes as they waved from the kitchen window.

The following day, on a tip from Helen Moncrieff, we
met with a man who had a remote cottage on a headland
of the mainland. Bob Spanswick had renovated his 'butt
'n ben', a two-roomed croft house, to a wonderful standard, sticking to traditional methods as far as he was able,
which included chimney stacks made, rather alarmingly,
out of timber and pitched tar. But it was the location of
Bob's house that completely captivated me. The approach
was via private road, the last stretch of which ran along
a shingle beach. The spur of land on which the house
perched was low-lying but bordered by jagged rocks that
all reeked of otter. Seals rested on small rocky islands just
off shore, and behind the house was a freshwater loch graced
with almost surreal perfection by a pair of whooper swans.

We were invited by Bob to join him with a cup of coffee
and to taste the soft spring water he drew from the well
beyond his back door. He told of the family that used to
live in the house full time and how they had saved their

young cousin from near certain death during a particularly savage winter storm. The waves from the raging sea had broken clean over the roof of the house and showered the building with rocks. The young girl was pushed by her parents through a tiny window in the back of the house to the relative protection of the walled garden behind, just as an immense boulder was hurled into the east-facing wall, collapsing the building where the girl would have been lying in bed. Bob's kind offer to allow us to stay in his house from time to time was gratefully received, but I knew we would be spending at least part of our time here through the harder winter months and knew too that this story would play on my mind when Savannah was with us.

We eventually found a splendid rental cottage on the west side of the mainland, not far from Walls. It was not where we wanted to end up, but it would certainly give us a comfortable base and the facility to check other houses more thoroughly once I returned with Marguerite and Savannah in a few months' time. There were otters on the doorstep, and the promise of summer Shetland specialities like red-throated divers hunting the bay in front of the house. A small beach nearby would provide a fabulous playground for Savannah.

At the end of a rushed four days, during which Charlie and I explored the northern isles of Yell and Unst too, notching up our otter count and calling in on more of Charlie's friends, I had a good idea of where I wanted to concentrate my otter-watching efforts. We had established where we would be based for the near future at least. I had also made some friends and contacts that would prove to be enduring.

On return to England, and with the detail of my film proposal rather firmer, I revisited Tim Martin, the series editor of *Natural World*, with a view to finalising production details.

Tim greeted me at the door of his office in the BBC Natural History Unit in Bristol. 'Hi Simon. Sounds like the recce went well. I've been up to London, and they wonder if this project would make a series rather than a one-off.'

I hadn't really considered that it might, but now it was mentioned, a series would allow greater scope to include other elements of life in Shetland beyond the pure natural history, particularly our own family life through the changing seasons. Over the following few weeks, I attended a number of meetings in London, prepared programme treatments and discussed possibilities with potential team members. A series it was, then, to follow the wildlife and our family through the four seasons on the Shetland Isles. It would be called *Simon King's Shetland Diaries*.

And then we received a very personal body blow.

I look back at the spring and early summer of 2008 as though through a gauze; it seems like a period lived by someone else. I was a bystander in my own life due to a major upheaval in our world. In the middle of April, Marguerite's mother unexpectedly passed away. Shockingly, less than a month later, her eldest brother also suffered an untimely death. The emotional blow to all of us, but particularly to Marguerite of course, took the wind out of our sails. My presenting another series of *Springwatch* that year was a surreal experience; watching the wild wonders of Speyside through the weekdays and paying my respects to my lost relatives at the weekend. When *Springwatch* was over and the time came for Marguerite and me to make the journey to Shetland, we were emotionally and physically exhausted.

Despite the upheaval, though, we both felt that we should carry on with our plans to spend the summer in the north. We would be together with Savannah, we would have time and space to reflect (or so we thought) and we would be sufficiently removed from some of the harsh details of our loss to allow us some healing time. On reflection, Marguerite's strength was nothing short of superhuman. Despite the turmoil and sheer enormity of everything she was going through, she remained supportive and positive about the prospect of going to Shetland. It humbled me.

Before we knew it, we were preparing our kit for the journey north, with little time to begin to adjust to what it was we were going through and the journey we were about to embark on. It was late June, and I felt that we should take the ferry to Shetland from Aberdeen rather than fly the whole way. The sea state should be fine, it would be a more human pace of travel and it would allow us to bring our own vehicle filled to the brim with our gear. It was the right decision, not just from a practical but also from an emotional point of view. The bubble of being on board ship gave us a little time and space to be alone, and for the sense of how far away we were going from the rest of the world to sink in. The ferry run lasts fourteen hours from Aberdeen, pausing briefly in the middle of the night at Kirkwall in Orkney. Fourteen hours during which we played with Savannah, enjoyed a splendid meal in the ship's restaurant and retreated to the cocoon of our cabin to sleep, lulled by the throb of the engines and the gentle pitch and roll of the ocean. The womb-like atmosphere was both comforting and restorative, taking us away from mainland Britain, away from some of the painful immediate truths of our world, and into a new adventure.

Arrival in Lerwick on the overnight ferry from Aberdeen is the single best way to expose yourself to Shetland, whether on your first visit or if you are a regular visitor. For a start, you get some sense of how distant it is from mainland Britain. But perhaps more importantly you are gently introduced to the islands from their southern tip, as you glide alongside the east coast before reaching Lerwick, which lies a little under halfway up Mainland.

I woke at six in the morning with the sound of the ferry's engines urging me to turn over and catch another forty winks. Pulling myself out of my slumber, I told Marguerite that I was going on to the deck, hastily pulled on some clothes and made my way up to the passenger decks. As I pushed open the heavy door to the outside world, I was greeted by a fresh breeze and grey sky, and a sea that was restless rather than angry. I walked on to the port side and was faced with a familiar sight from an unfamiliar viewpoint. Sumburgh Head, the southern tip of the mainland, drifted towards us as though we were the land mass and Shetland was on a southern migration. I immediately felt better, breathing in a sense of home-coming and calm.

I bolted back below decks, and helped Marguerite dress Savannah so that we might all greet the Shetland Islands together. Back on deck, we were joined by the small team who had travelled with and would be working with us for part of the coming month or so: Sam on camera, Jake on sound and Martin on production. Though Marguerite and I commonly work alone, illustrating our life as a family on this adventure would demand the help of others. I caught a glimpse of the high cliffs of Noss before the curtain was drawn across them by the southern tip of Bressay, but not before a few squadrons of gannets cruised by the ferry, well below our vantage point. Though Savannah was just a year and an half old, she was already doing well with her language or, to be more accurate, languages, since Marguerite speaks to her exclusively in French.

'Look at those big white birds, darling, they're called gannets.' I held Savannah up to get a better view.

'Gannets,' she echoed and I, predictably, felt a flush of fatherly pride. That's my girl!

Even the routine for arrival and disembarkation on the ferry is considered and humane. Rather than rush everyone off the ship as it docks at 7.30 in the morning, vehicle owners are asked to drive their cars on to the mainland, but can then return on foot to enjoy a leisurely breakfast in the ship's cafe. How very civilised.

Before heading to our rented cottage in the west, we made a supply run in town, stocking up in the local Co-op. As I made my way around the isles I was reminded once again of the confidence, sharing and friendliness of the people that had so warmed me when I first came to Shetland.

'Ay ay, how's it goin'?' 'Du found a house yet?' 'Back fur more otters?' 'I heard da killer whales have been seen again . . .' and so on. It was the antithesis of urban England where thousands of people can brush past you or squeeze together in public transport without recognising each other's existence. It was as though I'd been here for years and never been away; the most sincere and honest welcome I could have wished for.

Over the next day or so we settled in to our temporary home in the west and I set about exploring the neighbourhood. The house was situated about 200 metres from the coast, looking across a voe to the Isle of Vaila. I was bursting to check the neighbourhood for signs of otters, and so headed out early the next morning to scour the beaches and headlands for clues. Most otters in Shetland get their food from the sea. Even though the waters are cool, the marine environment is rich and varied and it is this, together with a lack of disturbance, that has led to such a healthy population. There are about a thousand otters spread around the hundred or so islands in the archipelago, which represents a good 10 per cent of the British population. Lots of otters then. All well and good, but an animal about the size of a large house cat, patrolling a stretch of rugged coastline that may be a couple of miles long, can be pretty tricky to spot. Fortunately, otters have a habit of letting you know they are in residence.

Within a few minutes of arriving at the coast below the house, I saw my first sign. A hundred metres ahead, the coast ran to a small rocky headland topped by a grassy bank, pretty with sea pinks nodding in the breeze. On a tussock close to the rocks, the grass looked particularly verdant and lush, as though a small patch had been carefully tended and nurtured by an elfin groundsman. My pulse raced a little as I approached this fertile garden, hoping my hunch was about to be proved correct. A careful scrutiny confirmed my suspicion. The deep green of the tussock was caused by months of extra nitrogen and other nutrients in the form of otter spraint.

As otters move around their territory, they regularly come ashore to mark it with heavily scented faecal deposits. It sounds revolting, but in fact these little patches of goo are manna for an avid otter-watcher. They often contain fish bones and scales, and once you get your eye in you can tell how old they are and so get a pretty good idea of when the sprainting point was last used. But most importantly they possess one of the most distinctive scents in the animal kingdom. You could blindfold me, take me halfway round the world and then ask me to identify otter spraint by sniff test alone, and I would be certain of my answer. This is where we really need one of those 'scratch and sniff' cards that were so popular in the late 1980s, but in the absence of that, I'll just have to resort to the word-mine. For a start, otter spraint does not smell bad. Honestly. In fact, I really like it. I have considered starting a new scent range for men, leading with an aftershave called 'Spraint'. It has a certain ring to it, if you'll forgive the pun. I can see the advertising campaign now: a deep, growling bass guitar, a rugged-looking chap striding over a windy headland. He meets a beautiful girl who swoons into his arms and a gravelly voice declares: 'Spraint . . . for men who walk on the wild side.'

So it's definitely not yucky. In fact, if you sniff something you think might be an otter spraint and it is unpleasant, then it's more likely to be the scat of a mink. Otter scent is like a mixture of violets and wet, fresh-cut hay, with a hint of the sea and a splash of musk. There is a distinct sweetness to it that persists for weeks, even months after it has been deposited.

Telling the age of a spraint is a bit more tricky. It depends of course on the weather to a certain extent, but a broad rule of thumb is that the wetter and 'stickier' it looks, the fresher it is. Spraint is delivered with a certain amount of mucus. When this is very fresh it creates small bubbles on the surface of the deposit. As time passes, these bubbles leave little craters as they burst. A spraint deposited at, say, five in the morning and discovered within twenty minutes will have loads of whole bubbles on it. After an hour, many of these bubbles will have burst, and, depending on how wet the conditions are, the whole thing will have started to dry on the surface. After two or three hours it will be more viscous and glue-like than watery. Drying continues until, after a week or so, it is entirely desiccated, and will crumble between your fingers. It retains its distinctive scent though.

I know all this because I have spent hundreds of hours sniffing otter spraint, and probing it with little sticks. I once watched an otter leave a deposit on a rock and I decided to first sit next to it for an hour or so, then continue visiting the spot throughout the rest of the day and ultimately, from time to time, through the week, so that I could build up a reliable first-hand knowledge of spraint-ageing. Weird perhaps, but super useful when it comes to spotting otters.

And the point of telling you all this is . . . the spraints that I found on the grassy knoll below our house were at least two days old.

A bit disappointing really. I also thought they were made by a single otter, rather than a family, since the age range was quite consistent and always in single marks rather than clusters of two or three, as I'd expect to see if a mother with cubs had marked the spot. I even hazarded a guess that it was a male that had made them. Nearby was a patch of soil that had been scraped bare. I have watched male otters scrape the ground with their claws after leaving a spraint, but rarely seen females do the same. So, I probably had at least one male otter patrolling this patch of coastline from time to time, but nothing too recent. I was mulling over the details of this detective work when my concentration was interrupted by one of the most evocative and melancholy sounds in nature. I knew instantly what it was that was responsible for the sound, but nonetheless the hairs rose on the back of my neck. Drifting to shore on the breeze from somewhere in the middle of the voe was the call of a red-throated diver.

As far as I'm concerned there are birds, and then there are super-birds. Sparrows are birds. So are herring gulls and carrion crows. Don't misunderstand me: I like birds. All are fascinating, engaging and charming in their own way. But super-birds have that something extra. Even though peregrine falcons are now quite numerous in the UK, whenever you see its anchor silhouette slicing across the sky, it brings a flush to the cheeks, a fizz to the veins, a shortness of breath. When a great spotted woodpecker lands on a bird feeder in your garden, even if it does so every day, it draws the eye and focus away from the blue tits and finches. It steals the show. Great spotted wood-peckers and peregrines are super-birds. So are red-throated divers. It's not just they are rare – about 1200 pairs breed in the UK of which a third are in Shetland – though rarity does give them an honorary subscription to the super-bird club. But just being rare isn't enough. I once saw a couple of Lapland buntings on the coast of Somerset. Definitely a rarity and for a while I got caught up in the whole 'twitching' thing, where seeing a rarity in Britain is the driving force behind a day's birdwatching. But after a little while, very pleasant though these small, sparrow-like birds were, it was clear that they were not in the super-bird category. Sparrowhawks, on the other hand, are common over most of the UK (though not in Shetland, as it happens), but their burning yellow eye, mercurial nature and dashing, secretive lifestyle puts them firmly in the 'super' category.

Everything about the red-throated divers is awesome. In summer plumage, their head and neck looks to be made of the softest velvet rather than feathers. The grey across the crown and face gives way to a designer flurry of bold black lines that run down the sides of the neck to the breast. Beneath the chin, and spilling down the front of the neck, is a deep burgundy blaze that gives the bird its name. The back is an unremarkable mottled grey-brown, but it is the eye that captivates me. Only when you see a red-throated diver at very close quarters, which in itself is tricky since most are quite nervous birds, can you fully appreciate the impossibly deep scarlet of their staring eye. It is as though they had built up a blind fury and were set to burst. It gives them a crazed, intense aura that is matched by their serpentine movement and flighty nature. But the last element that puts them firmly and unequivocally into the super-league is their voice.

If there is one sound to conjure up the essence of wilderness, of endless horizons and stormy seas, it is their call. It starts with a fluty, cat-like wailing, as though the wind itself had conspired with the sea and the hills to lift music from its heart. More often than not, the calls are conducted as a duet by a mating pair, and these wails roll over each other in a lilting cascade. As the excitement lifts, the intensity of the calls rises until one, then both, break into a guttural trilling that carries over a huge distance. And then, quite suddenly, the performance is over, and the wind sweeps the last of their refrain away.

That's what I heard from the sea in front of our house. That's when I truly felt I had returned to Shetland.

# Chapter 6

## Perfect Playground

'Oh, oh oh loooooook at thaaaaaat!' I was standing in my birthday suit, dripping from a pre-dawn shower after a failed attempt to blast the fatigue from my eyes with cold water, and staring out of the bathroom window at the coast below the house. I talk to myself a lot; I am frequently the only person around who's listening, especially when I see something exciting. Two hundred metres away, but unmistakable, was the dark arrow of a swimming otter leaving its delta wake ten metres from shore.

'That's it, that's the fella I want to see,' I muttered as I scrabbled to jump into my clothes, clumsily pushing both feet into the same trouser leg and almost falling down the stairs in the process. Marguerite was planning to organise equipment and meeting potential child-minders later in the morning, so I didn't want to disturb her or Savannah. A vain hope as it turned out; a rampaging elephant would have been more discreet.

By the time I was out of the front door, video camera and tripod on my shoulder, there was no sign of my wild neighbour, but I had noted the direction he was heading and reasoned I could run ahead and hope to catch up with him. Part of my professional life involves carrying heavy equipment across difficult terrain for days or weeks

69

on end. The other part involves moving very little, standing in front of the camera and presenting live television programmes or sitting in hotel rooms writing scripts. I had just come from a project involving the latter. As a result, after a couple of hundred metres of jogging with a weighty backpack and tripod up hill, I was puffing like a grampus. (A grampus, by the way, is an old name for an orca, or killer whale, and if you ever hear these magnificent creatures exhaling and grabbing breath as they surface, you will understand the analogy.) When I reached the top of the ridge to the south of our house, I could barely see I was so short of breath. I tried to comfort myself with the notion that a few days of this would knock me back into shape. Just as I was about to feel sorry for myself, wincing at the stitch in my side and aching calf muscles, I saw the otter again, this time almost directly below me.

It's extraordinary how swiftly pain fades when there is something else to concentrate on! I waited for the otter to dive, then leapt to my feet – OK, heaved myself on to my feet, grabbed the rucksack and camera and started off down the hill to the sea. I was still a good hundred metres away, so did not have to be too wary of being spotted, but erred on the side of caution nonetheless and paused as it surfaced for a breath before diving again. Otters have modest eyesight, but can pick out a human form against the skyline, especially if it is moving. By staying low and still you are unlikely to be spotted, and when they dive and are under water you can move closer. It's like a game of grandmother's footsteps. This otter was diving for long periods: between forty seconds and a minute as opposed to the more usual thirty seconds or so. This added weight to my guess that it was an adult male, since they often seem to dive for longer than females, probably as a result of their bigger size and resultant larger lung capacity.

I was soon crouching on the rocks that bordered the lapping tide, waiting for the next sign that the otter had surfaced. Nothing. A minute and a half went by and still not a sign. 'Blast!' I muttered. 'He must have given me the slip.' It is very easy to make the mistake of standing up to look around for an otter once you lose track of it, but it is almost always worth staying put for a few minutes at least before moving. They have a habit of melting for a while, then suddenly appearing within metres of where you are sitting. The water this morning was relatively calm, but a slight chop in the surface made it difficult to be certain of the otter's movements. And then he was back, this time swimming purposefully south again. His broad head and muzzle confirmed he was indeed male as he swam by, no more than twenty metres away.

I scanned the coastline in the direction he was swimming. Not good. What I had hoped for was a low peat bank – which would hide my outline – bordering a beach made of small rocks or shingle. Instead I was faced with a jumble of large rocks that ran steeply up to a grassy bank. The only way I could keep up with the otter now would be to walk on the grass, and that would put my silhouette against the skyline. Alternatively I could loop inland, run ahead and see if I could catch him coming round the headland towards me. Once he dived again, I plumped for the latter. After another run of four or five hundred metres that once again made me painfully aware of my lack of fitness, I set up in a rocky outcrop and scanned the water to the north. I saw him surface some fifty metres away with what looked like a large fish and start swimming in to shore. This is just the sort of moment you hope for as a wildlife film-maker; capturing on tape the otter out of the water and feeding would be a great start to our trip. But it was not to be. Once he reached the shore, the dog otter quickly disappeared from view behind large rocks where he obviously settled to feed. I considered stalking close to him to try and get a view, but decided not to risk disturbing him and waited, hoping I would spot him return to the water. After about twenty minutes I caught sight of a flash of a thick muscled tail flicking into the sea and realised he had had his fill and was now heading north along the shore, back the way he had come.

'Double blast!' I hissed as I got my gear together and ran inland to high ground again to try and pick him up. I spotted him swimming purposefully away along the shoreline and knew from his manner that this feeding bout was over and he was heading somewhere for a rest. I cut my losses and rested my gear on the ground. It had felt like no time at all had passed, but I had already been on the trail of this otter for over an hour. I had to take stock of the situation rather than be carried away by the sight of my favourite subject right on my doorstep. The fact was, I had to admit, this was not a great bit of coastline to film otters. Super for watching them at a distance, perhaps, but a number of topographical features made it very tricky to get reliable contact with any I might spot. The lack of beaches and proliferation of large rocks meant that when they came ashore there was a very strong chance they would be hidden. The steep bank running straight to the sea without a peaty overhang made it very tricky to camouflage my outline. And after a little more walking I discovered that, though beautiful, the coastline grew every more cliffy and rocky the further south I went. This wouldn't deter the otters, but it would effectively make it impossible for me to stay near enough to the shore to get close views of them. I would have to look elsewhere to find a better spot for filming them.

Having decided this, I felt somehow lighter, and started back for the house. As I crested a rise, I noticed in the distance the bold, distinctive forms of gannets plunging into the sea. I trained the camera on them, the telephoto lens acting like a telescope, and marvelled at their head-long plunges. The flock grew, other birds drawn to what must have been a good-sized shoal of fish, until more than thirty were circling over the water at a height of about twenty metres. Now, when one folded its wings and tilted towards the surface, others followed. At a distance it looked like an immense hailstorm, a white bar of birds collapsing into the ocean. A fitting avian curtain-fall on a lovely morning, and all before breakfast!

Whilst it may not have been ideal for filming otters, the coast in front of the house was a perfect playground for Savannah. A small, rocky beach was exposed at low tide, revealing a mosaic of rock pools and crestfallen weed, and this was the focus of any time I had available to share with my little girl. We would wander, hand in hand, down the pasture that gently sloped to the sea in front of the house. Our route took us past 'Lucky', a lamb that had fallen into the sea when it had tried to follow its mother to graze on steep cliffs. The ewe had perished, but Lucky had been spotted standing on a barely exposed rock that was sure to be covered at high water. A rescue mission was mounted and the lamb was now being hand-reared by the local crofting family. His familiarity with and dependence on man meant he shadowed us as we passed by, bleating the whole time, hoping for an extra milk feed.

Once on the beach, it became our entire world. I turned rocks and Savannah spotted whatever life lurked beneath. Crabs were a firm favourite, especially little hermit crabs that miraculously emerged from their adopted shell homes to scuttle around the bottom of her bucket. Anemones captivated her too, looking like nothing more than a blob of red jelly when above water, but slowly blooming into living florets once they were submerged. These simple connections with the natural world are, I believe, valuable beyond measure, and were one of the reasons I maintained a passion for natural history. I grew up in the late 1960s and 1970s, a period when most children still walked to school and were encouraged to play outside at every opportunity. I had the freedom to explore my local woodland, where parental words of caution and the occasional curfew were the common-sense measures that ensured my wellbeing.

We now live in an age where perceived dangers are creating a generation that is disconnected from the real world. We are bombarded with images of horror and fear; of murder, molestation and malevolence. Children are driven the few kilometres to school, and herded into activity groups that decide for them what will happen next in their lives, rather than allowing their imagination to take flight and find its own path to serenity and contentment. Shopping centres, computer games, television, iPods – all of them occupy the senses to the exclusion of everything else. Kids travel in cars playing hand-held computer games, never looking out of the window once on a journey that may take hours. Whatever the weather, young people – and many older – spend their days in an artificial bubble of human construct. Boredom – good old constructive boredom – is considered untenable. Every waking hour must be spent preoccupied with images, activities and sounds that force the individual to be outside themselves, rather than within.

I watched Savannah stumbling on the rocks, slipping on the seaweed and struggling to lift rocks with the warmest glow of recognition. Her feet were wet from sea water lapping over the top of her wellies, her hands were icy from fumbling in the rock pools and her smile was broad and fixed.

'Crab, Daddy,' she yelled in her helium-high voice. 'Hold it?' she enquired, looking up at me.

I picked up the little shore crab and placed it in her open hand. It scuttled and tickled her palm, and a peal of giggles bubbled up from her chest.

'Again . . .' she implored, and again the little crab was put into her hand. After a few seconds more palm-tickling, Savannah, to my surprise, whispered: 'Put it back now.' She had put herself into the life and world of this miniature creature and her natural empathy had decided it was time for it to go back to its mummy.

I received the phone call whilst driving to Sumburgh Head, where the crew were waiting for me to join them to film puffins. I glanced down to see who it was trying to reach me and noted it was my friend and fellow otterholic John Campbell. Pulling the Land Rover into a lay-by, I returned his call.

'Simon, hi . . . I don't know if you're busy just now, but there's been a report of an orca hunting seals near South Nesting. I'm on my way there now; thought you might like to know.'

'Fantastic! Thanks so much, John. I'm on my way; I should be about twenty minutes. See you there.'

I knew from my visit to Shetland in 2006 that sightings of killer whales were few and far between. A hot lead like this just could not be ignored. I made a hasty call to the producer, Martin, and left a message on his voicemail apologising for the change of plan and letting him know where I thought I would be. Mobile phone network coverage is sketchy on Shetland, and there was every chance I would not be in communication once I reached Nesting on the east of the mainland.

The drive was frustratingly slow, and knowing how fast-moving and dynamic orcas could be, I held very little hope that I would see it once I arrived at its last reported location. As I neared the stretch of coast where I understood it might be, I saw John running up the hill from the coast and gesturing to me to come, and come quick.

He greeted me at the side of the single-track road.

'Hi Simon, it's still here. A big bull. Apparently it got a seal about twenty minutes ago and it looks like it might try for another.'

I hurriedly parked the Landy off the road, scrabbled to get my kit together and then followed John at a trot down the hill to the rocky foreshore. As I neared the coast I spotted him. A vast, sail-like dorsal fin cut up through the grey water in the bay no more than fifty metres off shore. It grew, shining, black and imposing, until at its base the great bulk of the bull orca broke the surface to exhale and snatch a breath. Even at this distance I could hear the pneumatic explosion of respiration.

'Awesome John, thank you!' I panted whilst levelling the camera on the tripod, ready to film.

Close to shore, no more than twenty metres from where we were standing, I noticed a common seal in the shallows. It was an adult female, staring at us intently, but regularly craning its neck to look out into the bay. As I studied her through binoculars, I noticed a tiny pup between her and the shore. The youngster looked to be no more than a day or so old. This was why the orca was here. The stretch of coastline where the bull orca now lurked was a traditional pupping ground for the common seals. A number of tiny rock islands lay just off shore, offering the expectant mothers the ideal place to give birth.

Unlike their grey cousins, which have their pups on beaches in the autumn, on which the pups spend the first few weeks of their life, common seals give birth in summer, often on a rock that is covered by the sea at high water. As a result, the pups must swim when they are just a few hours old. Naturally, they are very vulnerable at this time, and, even in the weeks following their brutal baptism, they are inefficient swimmers, often resting their chins on their mothers' backs for a rest and diving for short periods only. To an orca, they represent an easy, if tiny, meal. That, of course, is on the proviso that they can be reached. The mother seal that I was watching clearly had previous experience of orcas. Despite her natural fear of man, she had decided that between the devil and the deep blue sea, she would take her chances with the devil – i.e. me – rather than risk the deep water and exposure to the orca with her newborn. Seeing her distress, I moved away from her a hundred metres or so before settling to follow the progress of the bull in the bay.

Much of the time, he seemed to be cruising aimlessly, keeping to a fairly tight circuit of an area of water lying between the furthest rocky island and the shore. From my work in Patagonia with orcas and the pioneering study that was currently being conducted by Andy Foote and Volker Deeke, I was reasonably confident that he was remaining completely silent and listening for the movement of seals in the weed and rocks below him.

I was joined by one of the very few people who live in houses overlooking the bay, who told me what had occurred forty minutes earlier. They had seen his fin in the bay, then an almighty commotion as his tail fluke had broken the surface with great force. After a couple of impressive splashes, the reason for the curious behaviour became plain. The massive predator thrust his tail at the surface again, but this time, he batted a half-grown seal clear of the water. I had witnessed similar behaviour with orcas killing sea lions in Argentina. It's not certain quite why they do this. It could be that, having snatched a seal from its hiding place, the safest way to dispatch it without fear of being bitten back is to beat it with their powerful tails. This is a real possibility, but it doesn't explain why orcas often continue the tail-beating behaviour long after their quarry is dead. It could perhaps be a way of flaying meat from bone, or tenderising a kill, but these notions seem fanciful for an animal that has very powerful jaws and rows of pointed teeth that should make short work of a young seal carcass. When hunting shoals of herring or mackerel, orcas use their tails to hit the shoal and then return to suck up the stunned fish. The truth is, no one yet knows why orcas use their tails this way with mammalian prey.

Our bull had eaten one seal and was looking for more. Once or twice he made sudden charges across the bay, the spray from his dorsal fin flying up and back as his speed tripled. I assumed he was sprinting at seals he had detected but, as far as I could see, unsuccessfully. After about twenty minutes I was joined by the rest of the crew, who had received my voicemail and wanted to try and record some in-situ material of me filming the orca. They arrived in time to see the bull, but only just. Soon afterwards he started to drift north along the shore and then headed out to sea. The last sign was the tiny clouds of his condensed breath catching the light in the distance.

Seeing a killer whale so early in our summer trip gave me a real sense of optimism about our stay here. We still had at least three weeks before I had to travel away from Shetland on another project, and there was every chance we would hear of more reports that orcas were hunting close to shore. But while orcas were a serendipitous bonus to our wildlife-watching stay, otters were the main reason I was here.

I had established that the otters close to the house we were renting would be very tricky to film, and so started to look further afield for a location that would give me a greater chance of close contact with them. We were soon to be joined by the specialist cameraman Charlie Hamilton James, who would be working with us for a few weeks to try and record images of us with the wildlife we were watching. Since our visit to the islands in February, Charlie and I had kept in close touch, discussing at length where best to focus our otter efforts. Before his arrival, Marguerite joined me on some coastal searches but, though we saw otters, conditions conspired to make the location unsuitable for one reason or another. When Charlie arrived in Shetland, a week into our stay, I had planned that we should have a meeting to discuss progress and then revisit some of the spots we identified in the early part of the year to assess levels of otter activity. As it turned out, that would have to wait.

# Chapter 7

## Killers' Return

'Hi Charlie. Welcome back matey,' I blurted into the crackling mobile phone. 'Now listen, I'm sorry about this, but they're back . . . The orcas . . . Yep, I've just had a call to say they're hunting just off shore at South Nesting again. I know you've only just landed, but I have to get down there as soon as I can. If you could get your kit together and join me, that would be great. See you soon.' Charlie had called me soon after his plane had landed at Sumburgh. He was, quite reasonably, expecting a gentle start to his two-week shoot with us, but had arrived just as I had received a call from a local naturalist, Brydon Thomason, letting me know that there was a group of orcas off the east coast. This time females and calves were reportedly in the gathering, and I couldn't ignore the opportunity to film them again, even though it was just days after my encounter with the lone bull.

When I arrived at Nesting, there was already a small gathering of people down at the coast. The presence of orcas always created a ripple of excitement with most Shetlanders, and those that had the chance tried to get out to watch them for the brief moments they visited inshore waters. I hastily got my camera kit organised and ran down to the seashore. Even as I trotted down the hill,

I could see that this was going to be very different from my encounter a few days earlier. At least two fins were showing above the surface, both of them belonging to females. A family party. As good as it gets.

'Looooook at thaaaaaat,' I exclaimed to myself as I set up the camera on a high promontory overlooking precisely the same bay that the lone bull had hunted a few days earlier.

The orcas were cruising close to the rocks, very slowly and with little apparent intent. Once again, I suspected that they were listening for the movement of seals in the shallows and, with the females being significantly smaller and nimbler than the males, they had a better chance of reaching seals that might have thought themselves safe. Two, now three, four, five orcas – females and their well-grown calves – kept surfacing for breath and then, among them, a great bull. I could instantly tell that this was a different animal from the one I had seen here previously by the shape of its dorsal fin and the grey saddle-mark on its back. At least six orcas hunting together within a couple of hundred metres of where I stood. That's enough to get even the most seasoned naturalist quivering!

When I first started my career as a wildlife cameraman, I would occasionally suffer from what is known in deer-stalking circles as 'buck fever'. Apparently, hunters who lack experience and are very excited by the prospect of shooting an animal often get the shakes just when they need them least. The adrenalin coursing through their veins as they raise the rifle to their eye has no natural release and their hand becomes too unsteady for them to take the shot. I well remember once trying to film wild ibex in the mountains of Spain, when I was eighteen years old and quite new to the disciplines of wildlife camera work. After a lengthy stalking hike up a hill, I finally managed to get a mature ram in my lens, and was preparing to roll film when I got the shakes. My hand on the panhandle of the tripod wobbled the magnified image so greatly that I had to lock off the tripod head and film the scene without touching the camera.

Since that day, I have managed to curb and control my excitement when filming so that I can hold a steady shot. But watching these orcas, so close to shore and in British waters, suddenly released the shakes in my hand for the first time in years.

'Stop it you twit,' I grunted to myself. 'Big dolphins . . .they're just big dolphins,' I whispered as a mantra to calm my enthusiasm.

Fortunately I got the wobbles under control in time to film a couple of females gently nosing around a rocky islet in beautiful sunlight.

With my attention so completely taken by the action on the water, I only noticed Charlie's arrival when he came puffing down the hill with his camera to join me.

'Hiya, Charlie. Not a bad way to be welcomed back to Shetland, eh?' I joked.

Charlie could barely speak he was so out of breath. I guessed he'd been working at a desk for the past week or so.

'I haven't seen them get anything yet. I don't even know if there are any seals left here after the bull was here the other day,' I added, concentrating again on the water in front of me.

As I did so, I saw the scythe-shaped dorsal fin of a female orca cruising straight to the rocks where Charlie and I were standing.

'Here comes one now,' I yelped unnecessarily.

The cow orca sank beneath the surface as she neared the rocks, leaving a V-shaped wake and large patches of still water where her powerful tail fluke had created turbulence. I thought that was the last we would see of her for a while, but then noticed to my astonishment that she was directly beneath us. I could clearly see her broad white eye-patch and her white underbelly through the calm water, as she rolled and looked up at where I was standing.

'Flippin' awesome,' I breathed. I was vaguely aware that Charlie was filming me, but any thought of pertinent and erudite comment was soon abandoned in the sheer impressive rarity of the moment.

And then she was off, twisting at a pace that suggested she was on to something or else had been called by one of her party.

She joined at least two other adult females close to the far rocks and together they began to cruise at a gentle pace again, pausing to dip their heads and listen from time to time. As they reached the northernmost point, I noticed a young seal coming up for breath no more than ten metres from the nearest orca. It was looking in completely the wrong direction and, were it not for the gravity of the consequences should this seal misjudge the great predators on its doorstep, it could have been very easy to see the comical side to the encounter. The pantomime chant of 'It's behind you' rang in my head, as the seal suddenly seemed to realise what was coming and dipped below the surface. No sooner had it done so than an orca surged into the view I had through the camera viewfinder in precisely the spot the seal had been.

'Is that it? Have they got one?' I asked myself rhetorically. I couldn't see how the little seal could have escaped the surging orca, but it was all so cryptic and tantalising.

The orca returned to deeper water and was joined by the others. And, once there, their behaviour changed. At first they all seemed to be having a meeting, huddled not unlike the way American footballers are before they make a play, with their heads bent into the centre of a circle to share information. I could not tell if they were searching for or sharing a meal. Then there was a sudden rush as one of the orcas broke away from the 'conversation' and sped across the open water. I tried to interpret what was going on as I filmed, and, having had the benefit of replaying the tape in slow motion later, was able to be certain. They had indeed caught the small seal and brought it into the centre of the bay. There they had almost certainly released it and re-caught it a number of times, watching it and then suddenly charging after it, just as a cat chases a mouse. Climactically, they had held it in their mouths and rolled with it on the surface before beating the little body with their tails. Finally, I assumed, they shared the small meal, dipping their heads and arching their backs at the surface. Surprisingly I saw no sign of blood, nor did any gulls hover over the scene to pick up scraps. The orcas' demolition of the seal pup must have been very thorough indeed.

As the orca pod left the bay and cruised out of sight to the north, I was able to greet Charlie properly.

'That was pretty awesome, eh? Well done for getting here in time. You must be shattered after such an early start.'

Charlie answered with a broad grin: 'I was, but I'm not now!'

Our plan over the next few days was to get back to our mission to find a suitable location to follow and film otters. Marguerite and I had employed the help of a local child-minder to look after Savannah for a period each day, and we were to work together as a team of three much of the time: Marguerite filming me and assisting with otter-spotting duties, and Charlie to follow with a telephoto lens to pick up shots of us working together. We were finding our feet with the team structure that could best chart our family life in Shetland, whilst at the same time follow our progress as wildlife film-makers, so the camera crew that had been with us for the first week or so were now heading back south.

Charlie and I had discussed the pros and cons of a number of known otter hot-spots and decided to plump for a little-visited patch of coastline on the east side of the mainland. It was not the prettiest of places, but it did tick many of the boxes we were looking for when it came to following otters. A large island was attached to the mainland via a narrow shingle causeway. This created an expansive bay between the island and the shore of the mainland and thus offered stretches of coastline we could walk along in virtually any wind direction without our scent blowing across the bay. Much of the shoreline comprised shingle beaches with few large rocks – ideal if an otter came onshore to feed; and low peat banks or shallow cliffs offered a backdrop that would camouflage our outlines once we were in pursuit of a swimming otter.

With the wind blowing from the east, we headed out on the rising tide to study the bay from the western shore. Charlie has exceptional otter-spotting skills and before long he declared, 'Got one . . . no two. On the far side, swimming south, close to the island.'

I studied the choppy water and, after twenty seconds or so, saw the brief flash of an otter surfacing about five hundred metres away.

'Well spotted . . . let's get over there, Charlie.'

Marguerite's task was to keep an eye on the otters and stay in radio contact as Charlie and I heaved our gear into the car and drove around to the far side of the bay. We could only get the car to within a kilometre of where we had seen the otters and had to run the rest of the way with our kit. The wind by now had shifted a little to the north, so we were able to run into the breeze, but risked a trail of our scent drifting over the water behind us. We had to be very careful not to over-take our target.

'Marguerite, do you copy?' I whispered into the walkie-talkie.

'Loud and clear. I lost them for a while, but they're

back where you saw them last, up on the rocks. They're playing together.'

I felt a sudden urgency to try and close the distance and broke into an ungainly trot. My fitness levels were at last returning. Charlie and I both guessed we were nearing the spot where we had seen the pair and decided to scramble down the low cliff to the beach below, well in advance of where they might be. Once we reached the exposed shingle it was clear that the bay ran in a convex arc, which meant we could not see around the corner.

'Wait here, Charlie. I'll creep forward and see if I can spot them.'

I stalked along the beach close to the cliff wall. As I reached the blind corner, I thought I saw the form of an otter in the water just off shore and suddenly felt terribly exposed. I ducked low and waited. There they were, just thirty metres away and coming towards me. When they dived beneath the surface I jumped up and made a dash for my camera.

'They're on their way,' I whispered to Charlie, who was already filming them. 'It's too late to move; we'll just have to hope they don't swim downwind.'

I crouched by my camera and spotted the first of them swimming even closer than before. As I filmed its progress it was joined by the second, and both headed directly towards me. A slow dawning of realisation came upon me. When I had stalked along the beach I had been vaguely aware that I had passed by a tiny freshwater pool that had collected at the base of the cliff. I hadn't stopped to check, but had clocked it as a good place for an otter to come ashore for a drink. That, of course, was precisely what these two had in mind.

'Blast,' I whispered, as it gradually became clear that we were within five metres of their drinking spot. We couldn't move now.

First one, then both otters swam and trotted with seamless grace from sea to land. The lead animal looked to be an adult female; she was followed by a very well-grown cub. Both hesitated in their passage up the beach to sniff the ground, then bounded towards the drinking spot. As the female reached the point where moments before my feet had crunched through the shingle, she stopped abruptly, as though she had walked into an electric fence. Then she spun on her heels and bolted for the sea, almost bumping into her cub, which was following her lead.

I had a dreadful sinking feeling. We had not been at this spot for more than a few hours and I had startled the very creatures I was hoping to get to know. A timid wild animal that has caught a hint of human scent will be on guard, looking for the owner of the smell. If I moved in the least I ran the risk of catching their eye, so I did not attempt to pan the camera on to the water to follow them. Instead I tried to watch their progress without moving my head.

Surprisingly, rather than disappearing leaving no more than a trail of bubbles, they both floated a few metres off shore, staring back at the point where they had sniffed my footfall. From their position, neither Charlie nor I would be seen against the sky, and the wind was still in our favour, carrying our scent along the shore behind us.

The mother otter had clearly caught a whiff of human from the track I had left, but she was not at all sure where that human might be. All four of us remained perfectly still for what felt like an age, until the female took a breath and dived, followed by her cub. I could tell by the way she left the water's surface, with a pronounced duck dive, flicking her tail in the air, that she had relaxed and was not swimming away to hide from us. She must have decided that we were long gone from the scene and had decided to go back to hunting. After twenty seconds or so she resurfaced with a butterfish in her jaws and chewed it noisily as she floated and trod water. Moments later her cub joined her, empty jawed, and tried half-heartedly to snatch a bite from his mother's meal. We were in luck. I had startled her, but not irrevocably so. The pair drifted past us and out of sight around a bend in the coastline.

I turned to Charlie. 'That was too close. Still, I think we got away with it.'

Charlie whispered back: 'Let's go inland and see if we can catch up with them.'

For the rest of the afternoon we kept track of the pair. Marguerite came around to join us and got some of the best views of otters she had to date, when the cub brought a meal to shore no more than fifteen metres away from us. This was going to be a very good place to follow otters.

Having settled on our otter-watching spot, we turned our attention once again to where we would base ourselves for the year.

The house we were renting was comfortable and in a

lovely location, but not really as wild as we had hoped for, and not ideally positioned for filming otters or other wildlife. We looked into several other options, including small cottages that were available for short-term rent, called böds, and even entire crofts that were for sale, until we heard of a house in the north of the mainland that might just suit our purposes. The tiny crofter's cottage in Northmavine had recently been given a new roof by its owners. Despite the remote location, it had mains electricity and running water and – over and above its 'mod cons' – the spot it occupied was wild and breathtaking. Perched on a slope above a narrow voe, it looked across hills to the south and out to sea to the west. Vehicle access was only possible via a beach at low tide. Thereafter, a steep climb up a hill brought you to the five-roomed house – living room, kitchen, two bedrooms and a small upstairs bathroom. Living here would be quite basic, but what the property lacked in ease of access it made up for in spades with its location.

A quick walk along the surrounding coast revealed several piles of fresh otters' spraint, and a five-minute binocular scan of the bay below the house added red-throated diver, puffin, shag, fulmar, oystercatcher and common seal to the list of species that could be seen from the front garden! Once inside, I swiftly discovered that I was either built differently from people in Shetland a hundred years ago, or else lacked their spatial awareness. An enthusiastic run up the steep staircase led to me drilling the top of my head into the ceiling once I reached the top. The ceiling height and head clearance through the doors was ideal for Savannah, though.

The owners of the house wanted no rent, but agreed after discussion to our helping to make the place a bit more comfortable in return for its use when we were in Shetland: a very generous and kindly offer on their part.

It would take a week or so to get organised for the move, but in the meantime we could continue to explore the area around the house and build up a greater knowledge of the wildlife in the neighbourhood.

I was especially keen to get a better idea of the otter population on my doorstep and, together with Charlie, decided to stake out the north shore to this end.

Our vigil started before dawn, which in midsummer at this latitude is at stupid o'clock! We came prepared for the long haul, with enough food and water for the day, along with clothing to accommodate any conditions, which, as it turned out, was entirely appropriate. I had quietly nurtured the thought that, though we were prepared to wait it out, we would have some positive views of otters within a few hours of dawn and that would lead to us cutting the endurance test short.

After seven hours with both of us scanning the bay below, during which the temperature shifted from 'very chilly I could do with another jumper' to 'blimey, I didn't know it got this hot in Shetland' weather, we still had not seen a sign of an otter. We had watched a red-throated diver fishing below and, from our vantage point, with the water clarity excellent, were able to chart its progress under water. It was clear that it was targeting small shoals of fish that we took to be sand eels, the dark mass of swirling bodies pierced by the darting dagger of a beak and torpedo-shaped body of the diver. Each time the diver started hunting, it was shadowed by a puffin, which kept a respectful distance, but made the most of the panicked fish to snatch a meal for itself. All fascinating and wonderful stuff, but still not an otter.

By midday, I was beginning to feel the effects of the three a.m. start, and decided with Charlie that we would take turns in keeping watch, with me taking a power-nap first. No sooner did I lie back in the short grass than I was sound asleep. I don't even remember getting comfortable, which explains my completely dead arm when I was awoken some forty minutes later by a dream in which Charlie was shouting something to me. I slowly worked out that he was yelling 'orcas', then rather more swiftly worked out that it was not a dream at all, but Charlie was in fact shouting, 'Orcas! Wake up!'

I sat bolt upright and attempted to stand, and promptly fell over again, both legs being as dead and completely useless as my arm from a lack of blood supply caused by my twisted sleeping position. I crawled to my camera with the first tingle of what was going to be a monumental pins-and-needles session in both feet, just in time to see the fin of a bull orca break surface in the bay below, close to the mouth of the voe. It was accompanied by at least one female, and both animals seemed to be hugging the shoreline, close to the rocks, undoubtedly looking for seals.

'Blimey Charlie! What are they doing all the way in here?'

'Dunno. But they just appeared out of nowhere. There they go!'

As Charlie pointed at the far side of the bay I saw the

bull orca surface again, but he had already turned away from the bay below us and was heading back out to sea. The cow soon took a breath close to where we had seen the bull and it was clear that the pair were not going to come into the shallower water of the bay below us. We managed to snatch a shot or two of the pair before they left, but as quickly as they arrived they were gone, nothing more than a rippling flat patch of water betraying their tail thrusts beneath the surface.

'Orcas . . . Blimey!' we both uttered in unison. Still no otters, but this was turning into quite a day for aquatic wildlife.

The afternoon wore on. Charlie had his nap, unbroken by any unexpected cetaceans, and woke to find me staring somewhat glazed out to sea.

'Still nothing,' I murmured unnecessarily.

The 'nothing' lasted another few hours. Enough for the sun to set, and the light to start dipping. Really late. I couldn't believe it. I had found so much fresh sign of otter on the shore below the house that I had been confident that we would see something in a day. But almost four-teen straight hours of watching had yielded killer whales, red-throated divers, puffins, guillemots and razorbills, and a smattering of other seabirds, not to mention the ubiquitous rabbits and ravens, but not even a sniff of an otter in the flesh. Reluctantly I stood and started to de-rig the camera, putting it into my backpack for the hike back up the hill to the house and car.

It always astonishes me just how often wild animals have a way with clichés. Just as I did up the zip and pulled the bag on to my back, I saw it. In fact, we both spotted it at the same time: the unmistakable delta ripple emanating from the head and shoulders of an otter, swimming out into the bay from the rocks beneath us.

'Flippin' typical,' I hissed as I pulled the zip open on my bag and hastily replaced the camera on the tripod. Charlie was already filming the otter by the time I got my lens to it.

'Looks like a dog,' he whispered. 'Big fella.'

'Yup. Lazy bugger too!' I added.

But at last we had the local otter in our sights. Perhaps we had just caught him on a bad day, but alarm bells began to ring for me that he might have a tendency to this crepuscular behaviour, making it very difficult to keep track of him with any consistency. We decided to try and follow him, despite the rapidly failing light, and ran inland to ensure our scent did not reach him. By the time we had both reached a promontory downwind of his fishing spot, he had caught something large and was swimming to shore beneath us. Alarm bell number two rang loud and clear. The coastline here was a jumble of large boulders. Try as we might, we could get no clear view of him once he was ashore. At one point I thought I could hear him chewing on his fish supper, but with the light against us, and the chances of a good view minimal, we decided to pull out.

Sitting on the top of the hill, we reflected on the day's progress.

'It's a stunning spot, but it's going to be very tricky to follow the otters here,' I offered, more as a confirmation of what we were both thinking than any kind of illumination of the day's work.

'Yup,' agreed Charlie sagely.

I still had not moved into the little croft house, so had a long hike and drive back to our rented property in the west before I could call it a day. After almost twenty hours of effort, I had come to a couple of conclusions. Filming otters at the new house was going to be difficult, if not impossible. That was the bad news. The good news was that there was plenty of other wildlife in the area, and with the surprise (and as it turned out unique) visit from the orcas, the potential for the unexpected. We would move in to the croft and I would travel to the otters on the east coast if I wanted to work with them. The croft would make a great base for Marguerite, Savannah and me, and for Marguerite and myself to film wildlife near home, and we would just have to make the journey east for consistent views of otters. A good compromise.

# Chapter 8

## Moving In

Before getting back into the rhythm of filming the wildlife, I had another duty – or more an ambition, really. The croft was grazed by a small flock of Shetland sheep and, with the days long and relatively warm, the time had come to shear them. In Shetland, as on most farms in the British Isles, this was carried out by contractors for the most part: men with a strength of arm and precision with the clippers that could make short work of a large flock. Even though the croft flock numbered only forty or so, a contractor would be carrying out the work here too, but it was usual for the croft owners to assist – both in the management of the flock and by taking on some of the shearing itself by hand, to speed up the process.

That's where I came in. I had helped to look after Shetland sheep in the south of England, and had even owned three wethers (castrated rams) to graze the orchard at the house I used to live in on the Somerset Levels. I had helped with shearing, though not for many years, and my knowledge of the art was worse than sketchy. It was so much a part of life here in the summer, though, I wanted to help in any way I was able, and so it was agreed that I would meet the house-owners and the contracted shearer at the property. Of necessity, a dry day was chosen (shearing wet sheep is a thankless and unproductive task) and as Marguerite, Savannah and I drove along the beach to the house, we could see that already a number of sheep had been herded into a small pen at the top of the hill.

'What can I do to help?' I asked Chris, the croft owner, once we had reached the sheep pen.

'We still have a few to get in, if you could help with that please, Simon.'

Together with Savannah, Marguerite and the owners' collies, we did our best to prevent any sheep from bolting downhill as they were guided towards the holding pen. Savannah was particularly good at winning the sheep's confidence by bleating at them. She also developed a curious obsession with their droppings and kept gathering hand- fuls of the stuff in various stages of desiccation.

By the time we had the entire flock safely enclosed, Savannah's pockets were chock-full of sheep poo and I was already puffing from the effort of running up and down the hill, but still keen to get stuck in to the real business at hand.

'Any chance I could shear a few of them?' I asked a little sheepishly. Sorry.

'Of course, Simon. Have you done it before?'

'Not for twenty years, and even then I just helped out.' This was true. Twenty years earlier I had helped out with shearing. I had even had a go at clipping a sheep with hand shears, though had never quite got the hang of it. In fact, I'd never rid a sheep of its entire fleece, pulling out of the task halfway through for fear of snipping off something vital.

'If you could just refresh my memory, please?' I asked Amelia, who owned the croft with Chris.

She immediately came to my aid, showing me how to hold the ewe on her back and, using the lethal-looking hand shears, to clip the fleece close to the root whilst pulling it just enough to expose the under-fleece but not so much that the skin stretched and was in danger of being cut. She made it look terribly easy, finishing an entire fleece in about five minutes or so. Once released, her newly trimmed sheep leapt to its feet with renewed vigour and a spring in its step. How hard could it be?

My first victim, and I use the word appropriately, was a lovely creature, steady in character and mature enough to know the routine. Little did she know the routine was to be somewhat changed this year by an eager novice.

I set to the clipping with concentration and commitment, taking great care to avoid the ewe's flesh. With the dagger-pointed shears in my hand and the oily lanolin from the fleece coating everything in seconds, I was acutely aware of just how dangerous this could be for my charge. If she struggled when I had the point close to her groin or udder, the consequences were unthinkable. I worked my way through the fleece very gingerly, pulling the clippers away every time the ewe wriggled in the slightest. Some ten minutes later I made the last cut to the back of the fleece and allowed the ewe on to her feet.

Unlike the sheep clipped by Amelia, or the six others that had been sheared by the professional help with the electric clippers, my ewe did not have a spring in her step. If anything, she was downright shaky, having been held in the prone position for so long. She was some-what short of looking neat and tidy, too: scruffy would be a kind description; a shambles more accurate. There was blood on her fleece too. My blood. In my determi-nation not to nick her skin, I had pulled the shears away rather too swiftly at one point in the proceedings and had gashed my own index finger, which then covered her and her fleece with vermilion. She joined the rest of the neatly shaven flock muttering something only a sheep would understand, but I have an idea of what it was she was saying.

I managed to shear three sheep in the time it took Amelia, Chris and Jonathan, the shearer, to finish clip-ping the entire flock of thirty or so. Towards the end my technique did improve, and I think I eventually managed to complete a fleece in less than ten minutes, leaving rather fewer 'missed bits'. I started to feel rather smug until, after completing my final fleece, I tried to stand up straight.

My back had seized up in a crouched hunch, my thighs had cramps, and I couldn't have opened a jam jar in my right hand after all the effort of squeezing the clippers. And that was just the start of the after-effects. By eight the same evening, my entire body felt as though I had been running a marathon with a sack of bricks on my back. I had pain in muscles I didn't even know existed. I tried hard to bluff my way through the agony I was in, feeling embarrassed by my lack of strength and stamina, but my true state was obvious from the way I tottered in and out of the car, or limply shook hands with everyone to say farewell. The next time I saw someone hand-shearing sheep, it would be with renewed respect.

Little by little we got the cottage equipped for comfortable, self-sufficient living, borrowing a livestock trailer from a friend to tow the refrigerator, beds and other heavy items across the beach and up the hill. Once the wood-burning stove in the kitchen had been running for a few hours and the open fire in the living room had chased the damp from the walls, it began to feel like home. Savannah loved the scale of the place, so well suited to her diminutive frame, and once we were curled up on the sofa reading stories before her bedtime, I felt a sense of wellbeing in the place. It had been home to a family not so long before our arrival, and I could imagine how calming and restorative time in this little cottage overlooking the sea must have been. Tough at times too, of course, but surrounded by natural beauty and a simple routine for warmth and sustenance. That was before we spent time there in the winter, of course, but for now it was idyllic.

It had been about a week since I had startled the mother otter and her well-grown cub on the coastline to the east, and I sorely wanted to reconnect with them, but this time I vowed I would remain invisible. Together with Marguerite and Charlie, we revisited the stretch of coast where we had last seen the family at dawn, and soon spotted them on the far side of the bay. After a short drive and a longer walk, we arrived at the stretch of coastline where we had seen them. It was close to the beach where I had inadvertently spooked them a week earlier, but a little further to the south, at a point where the coast rose up to a low cliff of loose rocks. I crawled on my belly to poke my head over the cliff edge, and before long spotted the pair, swimming and hunting about fifty metres off shore.

I decided to try and scrabble down the cliff to ensure that they would not see my silhouette, keeping the jumble of rocks against my back.

Each time they dived I made further progress down the bank, Marguerite keeping watch from a prone position near the top. When they surfaced I froze, regardless of my position on the descent. This meant holding the camera, the backpack full of kit and the tripod still, often in very precarious positions. As I neared the base of the cliff I could see that both otters were heading further south again, and would soon be out of sight around the next headland. Great. I'd just about reached a position where I could film them, and soon would have no view of them whatsoever.

Rather than rig the camera, I decided to cut my losses and climb back to the top of the bank, thinking that I could run inland and ahead of them to get a more prolonged view as they approached my new hiding position. There had been rain in the morning and stretches of the steep slope were slick with wet mud. As I reached the halfway mark on my ascent, the backpack I was wearing suddenly swung away from my body, threatening to unbalance me and topple me down the slope. To prevent the fall I threw my left leg out to try and counter the movements, and just managed to get purchase with my left foot on a small rock. It prevented my fall, but now my entire body weight plus the extra thirty kilos of camera kit were all resting on the one leg, which was itself at a jaunty angle. Something had to give. It was my knee. I immediately knew something very unpleasant had happened to the ligaments, but had no option but to bite into the pain. Once I regained balance and composure, I was able to hobble to the top of the bank. On the grassy slope I slumped into a heap.

Marguerite could see the look of discomfort in my face. 'Are you OK?'

'This flippin' backpack is loose. I almost fell off the cliff back there. I think I've knackered my knee.'

It wasn't broken, but the pain suggested that I had strained some of the ligaments, hyper-extending the joint in a direction nature had never intended.

'Just give me a minute. Would you and Charlie try to keep the otters in view, please? I'll be fine. I'll catch up with you in a bit.'

Marguerite wisely protested at my insistence that I could carry the camera kit and would be back on my feet in a few minutes, but also knew me to be pretty stubborn when it came to trying to keep up with the subjects I was following. Reluctantly she walked ahead with Charlie, taking a walkie-talkie with her to keep in touch with me. After five minutes or so her voice crackled over the handset I was holding.

'We've got them. They're both together about a kilo-metre to the south. You OK?'

'Well done. I'm on my way.'

I wasn't really OK. My leg hurt like stink, but I so

wanted to try and get some good views of the otters that I decided self-pity could wait. I had to take it slowly on the walk across the moor, though. My left knee, now weakened, kept bending in the wrong direction if I didn't concentrate on how I placed my foot, and more than once I collapsed in pain. By the time I caught up with Marguerite and Charlie, I was sweating more through the effort of fighting through the jabbing daggers in my leg than any physical exertion.

All thought of my leg evaporated once I saw the otters, though. Both were hunting on calm water not far from shore. Charlie and I scrabbled to a vantage point on a low cliff, while Marguerite filmed from a distance. The wind was in our favour and, though we were exposed against the skyline, we thought that the distance was sufficient for us to remain undetected. We didn't have long to change strategy even if we had wanted to, as the pair swam towards the shore where we now had our cameras rigged and primed. The water was so pure and wind so light that as the otters dived we could clearly see their progress beneath the surface. The normally hidden part of their world was suddenly revealed with astonishing clarity. In many ways the view was better than if we had been beneath the surface with them, since it seamlessly combined their progress on the surface with their subaqua movements. It further reinforced one of the reasons I find otters such engaging and compelling creatures to watch. They are masters of the elements they frequent, on land or in the water and, as they make the transition from one to the next, they don't miss a beat.

As they paddled on the surface, all four legs were at work, the tail more or less following in their wake. From time to time they paused and rolled, using their forelimbs to perform the manoeuvre and pushing with their hind feet to get moving once more. Just before a dive, they lifted their heads clear of the water to snatch a deep breath, then ducked beneath the surface again. Immediately their method of propulsion shifted: forelimbs tucked close to their sides, webbed hind feet spread wide either side of their tail, and their whole body rippling in a wave action that included their broad, muscular flattened tail. Their speed increased dramatically and their bodies glimmered with a sheen of air trapped in their coats, a long stream of tiny bubbles pouring out from their fur as it compressed with the pressure of the dive. They made their way directly to the sea bed, about two metres down, and nosed and twisted amongst the seaweed, using their forelimbs to power-thrust right or left to thoroughly investigate their marine world. At one point, the adult female surfaced directly below us, and on surfacing stared directly up at our position. We held our breath, expecting her to melt away into the distance, but instead she huffed a little, then dived and, followed by her cub, continued to hunt until she had disappeared.

'What terrific views,' I smiled across to Charlie. 'Looks like they might come ashore round the corner. Let's try and get there first.'

With Marguerite keeping watch from above, Charlie and I scrabbled down the slope to the water's edge some two hundred metres further along the coast, arriving in time to see the otter pair coming ashore eighty metres upwind of us.

'I'm going to sneak up there and see if I can get a view,' I whispered.

Charlie filmed my progress along the beach, but it was too risky for both of us to try and close the distance between ourselves and the now land-based otters.

I very slowly crept over the rocks to the point where the pair had disappeared from view, my knee now delivering a constant dull ache, but the adrenalin of the previous view and now the potential for a very close encounter banishing the pain to the back of my consciousness. I climbed a large rock, teetering with the camera kit on top as I scanned the low shore, now exposed by the falling tide. And there they were, or, at least, there was a tuft of hair belonging to an otter no more than fifteen metres away. I looked with my binoculars and could see the gentle rise and fall of the otter's breathing moving the fur up and down. If I could just shift another metre or so, I would have a clear view.

I gingerly crept across the top of the rock and, with every limb straining to maintain balance, shifted the camera to point at the rocks below me. At last I had them. Mother and cub were settling to sleep, fur drying to a pale brown fluff, rolling on their backs and sides in the bladderwrack to further dry their pelt. I was visible to the pair, but was lost to their view by the jumble of rocks all around. So long as they didn't see me moving, I could remain undetected. It was hugely tempting to try to rapidly get the camera into a position where I could film, but I dared not risk being spotted, so instead inched the tripod into position little by little over five minutes or so. By the time it was settled, the otters were curling up to sleep. I could see now that the cub was definitely a male, already bigger than his mother and, I guessed, about a year or more old. It would not be long before she became irritable and fed up with his company, but now they were still as close as they had been for the past twelve months, the cub nuzzling into his mother's soft pelt and she grooming his side and back with her incisor teeth. Like a young human child settling to sleep, the cub kept wriggling and twisting until he was comfortable, and then at last they lay still, feet touching, nose to tail.

Having filmed enough to make what I hoped would be an engaging sequence, I took my eye from the camera and settled as best I could to simply share their space. The joy of being in the presence of these creatures, so competent and adept in their environment, to relax knowing that they were oblivious to my presence and to share a private slice of their lives filled me with a sense of well-being and a glow of true happiness. Since my early infatuation with the Shetland Islands, as a dream wilderness that held the potential for moments of close empathy with the wild spirits of the world, I had hoped for this moment. And now it was here, it was everything I had imagined it could be, and more.

I lost track of time, the gentle lapping of the sea against the rocks on this near windless day acting as a metronome on a timeless moment. Each soft wavelet beat not a man-made second, but the inexorable shift of tide and sun, of heartbeat and breath from a mother and cub lost deep in their slumber. From time to time their toes twitched and nostrils flared, and I imagined their dreams chasing silver bars of fish through the gloomy depths, or perhaps playing games of chase in the surf. For a time I was with them completely, sharing their world, their dreams, their complete relaxation and calm.

The reverie was broken by the shrill call of a redshank that had rounded the bay to feed on the exposed shingle in front of me. Its beady bird eyes on the constant lookout for trouble, it had spotted me and been startled. The mother otter immediately lifted her head, alert and wary. Her sudden shift from deep sleep to sentinel reinforced for me how in tune these creatures were with their environment, how every detail of their world had a meaning, whether it was a shifting wind or an alarm call from one of their natural neighbours. Though the otters were still oblivious to my presence, the piping redshank was enough to have unsettled them, and they both stretched and yawned before slinking away from their resting place and down towards the sea. I didn't try to follow. I wanted to absorb the moment fully, to allow the magic of the encounter to sink in. So often we rush through our world, whether it be dashing through a city centre or jogging through a park, without stopping to absorb its detail. But when we allow the time to really get to know a place, to know its subtleties and changes of rhythm, we are the richer for it.

For the most part I carry with me the burden of being a human being. There are, of course, wonderful advantages to being a member of the species *Homo sapiens*, but on the downside we have a history of being one of the most dangerous creatures ever to have walked this earth, and this has a profound effect on most wild creatures we meet. As someone who is fascinated by the natural world, this is my greatest handicap, and I spend a good part of my life doing my very best not to let the rest of the world know what I am. But every once in a while, I shed my human form and become one with the place I am in and the creatures I am with. I am no more disruptive than a wren hopping through the rocks, or a patch of sea pink flowers nodding in the breeze. Until my cover had been blown by the redshank, I had found that place with the otters, and it was a moment I could never lose. The rock where they slept would remain in my mind's eye. I could imagine it still warm from their bodies, and every time I passed by it in the future it would warrant a glance to confirm whether or not they had returned.

# Chapter 9

## Sea Swallows

The summer was now in full swing, and with the long days came a bustling rush from virtually all living things, making the most of the season's bounty. Everywhere birds were raising broods; among them some of the most delightful of creatures in Shetland: the arctic terns. Shetland hosts over half of Britain's breeding population of these world travellers, and I wanted to feature a nesting colony in the film we were making. There are many gatherings of terns on quiet beaches around the shoreline and we decided to concentrate on one in a beautiful bay on the west coast, protected from the full force of the ocean by a fortress of jagged rocks. In the lee of this natural sea wall, a sweeping beach had formed, and it was here that the terns, about a hundred pairs, were nesting.

Even though terns are feisty birds and quick to settle after any disturbance, it was essential that I should introduce a hide to the scene to film from; this would have to remain in place for a few days so that the birds could become accustomed to it.

The hide went up without incident some ten metres or so from the nearest nest, and birds were settling back on their nests before I had a chance to leave the colony completely. Despite their indifference to the new structure in their midst, I still wanted to leave the hide for a day or so to be sure that every nesting bird was completely comfortable with it.

The day following our venture into the tern colony proved to be a breezy one. In Shetland, a breezy day is anything much below a storm force ten. Then it got windy. My thoughts were with the hide, or what would be left of it once I returned to try and film. I had used guy ropes and rocks to secure it against the wind, but as the strength of the gusts increased I grew increasingly concerned that it would not survive the battering. It was getting dark by the time the worst of the storm hit, and there was nothing I could do but hope for the best.

At dawn the next day the breeze had subsided. As I reached the tern colony it was clear that something had indeed happened to the hide. However well camouflaged it might have been, it was not invisible, but as I looked through binoculars at the spot I had erected it, there was no sign whatsoever of the structure. I had a feeling of dread. What if it had crashed through the colony, taking chicks and eggs with it in a tumbling rampage? Terns nest on the ground in nothing more than a shallow scrape, and their chicks and eggs depend for survival on camouflage and the defensive attacks of their parents against predators. They had no defensive strategy to deal with a large tent flying at them at sixty miles per hour.

Ten minutes later, I reached the spot where I had pitched the hide. A couple of broken guy lines and a jumble of rocks betrayed its former location, but that was all that was left. The terns nearby seemed in good shape, though.

Despite their constant screams of alarm at my presence, I could see that the closest nest scrapes still had chicks and a careful scour with binoculars revealed a nearby nest with eggs too. Where, then, had my hide gone? I estimated a likely flight line based on the wind direction of the past twenty-four hours and scrabbled over the rocks to the northwest of the colony in search of further clues. Another fifty metres further on, I came to a sea pool, and there, visible through the crystal clear water and wallowing like a giant camouflaged jellyfish, was my hide. It was twenty metres or so from the shore, and had collapsed like an umbrella, but looked to be otherwise intact.

'Right then. Better get it, I suppose,' I muttered as I whipped off my boots, socks and trousers. The sea around Shetland remains a fairly constant temperature – cold. It hovers at around fourteen degrees centigrade in late summer; that's a super temperature to encourage a proliferation of sea life, but cold enough to make a human being think twice about paddling. I didn't have much choice. I waded in to the pool and the bite of chill instantly made the skin on my legs feel as though it was shrinking. The rocks underfoot were invisible beneath a lush growth of algae, and very slippery, but I only got thigh deep by the time I reached the submerged hide.

Once ashore, I inspected the structure for damage, which was miraculously minimal, and after a spot of drying off, re-erected it by the tern colony. I then returned to the hill above the bay, where I was joined by Marguerite, who helped me carry the camera kit to the hide and act as a walk-away. The latter role is key to successfully convincing birds that a hide structure is safe. Most bird species can't count, or at least don't appear to be able to, and so two people arriving at a hide, and one 'walking away' usually convinces the birds that no one has remained hidden, and they settle more quickly.

By the time I had the camera rigged and Marguerite had started her journey back to the hill, the first of the terns was settling in front of the hide.

I get a curious feeling when working from a hide, one that verges on a voyeuristic pleasure. It may sound a bit kinky, but sitting in a dark little tent when a timid wild animal comes close to you of its own volition, completely unaware that you are watching, is a pulse-quickening thrill. I used to get a similar feeling as a young kid when playing hide and seek with friends, waiting in a wardrobe to be discovered whilst peeping out through a crack in the door at the seeker searching fruitlessly in the wrong place. When using a hide to observe or film wildlife, the relationship between the watcher and the watched is a biased one. The watcher is privy to the subterfuge, the watched ignorant of it. But the parallels between hide and seek and observing wild creatures are still pertinent, since a nervous wild animal is constantly on the lookout for danger, and if the hide is doing its job, you are fooling its senses and ducking past its survival tactics. If all goes to plan, you are the architect of an otherwise impossible encounter whilst leaving your subject completely ignorant of your subterfuge, and that is a singular thrill. The pleasure may stem from an ancestral hunting drive in our species; the adrenalin rush that comes when getting close enough to our quarry to deliver a killing blow. How much more delicious then, to savour and prolong the thrill of close contact without ever taking a life.

Within a couple of minutes, the tern colony had restored to calm and I had at least eight birds within ten metres of the hide with one pair no more than three metres away. Even with the naked eye I was able to admire the beauty and detail of these delicate fairies of the sea. Arctic terns are probably the most travelled creatures on earth, migrating every year to their northern breeding grounds which include, as their name suggests, Svalbard and other islands in the Arctic. Shetland is in fact one of their more southerly breeding strongholds. As the northern hemisphere starts to darken with the onset of winter, the terns head south, following the sun around the globe, to fish the cool waters of the sub-Antarctic and sometimes even reaching the Antarctic continent itself. If the journey were conducted in a straight line, it would represent a round trip of some 20,000 miles each year. But of course, the birds don't just fly to their breeding or wintering ground and then rest for a few months. A large section of their lives is spent on the wing, scouring the seas for small fish that they catch with a shallow plunge dive. The added miles that build up from day-to-day living must bolster the total notched up by each bird by a very considerable amount over its lifetime, which may be thirty years or more.

After a short while, the bird closest to my hide started calling excitedly and I assumed its partner was in the air nearby. Sure enough, a tern arrived with a small fish in its beak and hovered enticingly over the head of its mate, teasing it with the potential meal. After a few seconds of this astonishing display of aerial prowess, the arriving bird landed alongside its partner and pointed its beak to the sky, complete with fish, excitedly chattering the whole time.

'Come on, chum, stop teasing her,' I muttered under my breath as I filmed the display. She must have liked the element of suspense in her mate's seduction, though, because she too was chattering wildly, her wings drooping by her sides. Eventually, she leant forward and took the fish from his beak, brandishing it in a showy way for a while before swallowing it down. This was the behaviour of a couple with no family yet to raise and I thought that they must have lost their first brood to the weather or a predator and were having another go. It was leaving it pretty late in the season to be starting, though, since many of the chicks in the colony had hatched and one or two were at the point of fledging.

Just as I was considering what fate might have befallen the couple's chick or egg, the whole colony fell silent, then, as one, took off. The behaviour, known as a 'dread', sometimes occurs for reasons unknown, but it is also sometimes caused by the arrival of a predator. On this occasion it was the latter. After a few seconds of silence, the whole flock of terns erupted into a screaming, chattering mob. I strained forwards to identify the focus of their wrath and saw, low and purposeful in its flight towards the colony, a bonxie. As well as having a justly deserved reputation for being piratical, great skuas, or bonxies, are versatile and powerful predators. They can snatch cliff-nesting bird chicks from their nests, and I have seen them successfully out-flying and killing puffins, razorbills and guillemots. This bird was on the lookout for less demanding prey: arctic tern chicks and eggs.

You might think that the task would be simple, but with over a hundred adult terns screaming, pecking and defecating on its head, the invader was finding it difficult to concentrate. He made a couple of false landings close to what he must have thought was a meal, before eventually dashing between the rocks and appearing with a tern chick in his beak, held headfirst. The raid was dramatic, mercenary and very, very effective. Almost as soon as it had arrived, the skua had taken what it was looking for and was flying purposefully away back to its own nest and no doubt dependent youngsters, leaving in its trail an ever-diminishing flock of irate parent terns, like a stream of waste paper fluttering behind a dump truck. Within a few minutes of the attack the colony had settled again, but I reflected on just how vulnerable these tern colonies were to attack, despite the adults' fiery temperament in the face of a threat.

Not long after this incident, I had further reason to empathise with the fragile lot of the arctic tern. I had been working with the otters on the east coast, and was driving away from the coast when I stopped to say hello to the local landowner.

'Did you see the injured tern, Simon?' he asked.

'No. How dreadful! Where was it?'

He explained that he had seen it struggling on the

tide-line of a shingle bar, but had been busy with his sheep and unable to stop to try and catch it. He wasn't sure how bad the injury or illness had been.

'I'll go back and take a look,' I suggested, turning the car in a nearby gateway.

It was not long before I came across the sorry scene. An adult arctic tern was sitting close to the water's edge, at first glance looking perfectly well. But as it tried to take off it was clear that one of its wings was not functioning properly. I got out of the Land Rover and walked slowly up to the confused and frightened bird. It tried in vain to fly away; I carefully bent down to scoop it up, ensuring I held its wings tight to its body to prevent it from struggling too much. As I did so, it almost immediately seemed to relax, staring up into my face with its deep dark-brown eyes, not even attempting to peck me. I carefully extended the dysfunctional wing and my heart sank. A bone had shattered in two, both ends piercing the flesh so that the wing hung limply. Bleeding had all but stopped but the tern could only move its wing at the shoulder, the main part flapping uselessly. It was about as much use for flight as a loosely flapping sheet might be.

'Hello my little darling,' I said to it sombrely, looking around for what might have been the cause of the injury.

Some nearby low power lines were the most likely culprit, and I assumed the tern had unwittingly misjudged its flight path, twisting at the last second to avoid the wires and smashing its right wing at speed into the unyielding barrier. I knew from bitter experience that such breaks in delicate seabirds could rarely be fixed, but still wanted to seek advice. Perhaps modern veterinary technology had come on apace since my childhood dealings with injured birds?

After a few calls to very sympathetic experts in the field, from the SPCA to the RSPB, I had little reason for hope. All had said that the chances of a full recovery were extremely slim, and that for a bird that depends so absolutely on its astonishing aerial prowess, even the slightest defect would sign its death warrant in a slow and grisly decline to starvation. The wing could be amputated, and the bird would lead a life in captivity. But all, including myself, believed this to be too miserable a future to contemplate. To sentence the creature to a decade or more of solitary confinement, never able to express its innate desire to take to the skies, to follow the sun around the globe in an endless summer, was the worst of tortures. Nonetheless, I left messages with other experts in the field and put the bird into an empty cardboard tape box and drove it back to our little home on the hill. By the time I reached the cottage, everyone I had contacted had got back to me, and none of them had any more hope than those I'd already asked. The tern would never fly again.

Ultimately the decision was mine.

Taking the life of another living thing is not something I can do or ever have done lightly. I am a hypocrite in many ways, since I eat meat, eggs and cheese, all of which depend in some way on ending the lives of other creatures, even if it is the unwanted chicks from a chicken hatchery or unwanted male calves in a dairy farm. I rationalise these eating habits by trying my best to eat only animals (and their by-products) that have been raised in a humane, free-range environment. I also fish from time to time, and will, on occasion, keep my catch for my own supper. Here, too, I justify my actions as being an honest expression of my carnivorous nature and, though I undoubtedly enjoy the process of trying to catch the fish in the first place, having the incentive of a potential meal of a fully free-range fish at the end puts me closer somehow to the wild creatures I watch and film in my professional life.

Killing an animal is not something I can do without conscience, nor would I ever wish to. I want to care, to empathise, to consider the significance of my actions in this most profound of acts.

Taking the life of an animal to 'put an end to its suffering' is one of the hardest acts of all. The question of quality of life over life at any cost is, by definition, a subjective one. I could not ask the tern which course it would prefer, and were it sentient enough and given the capacity to answer, it would quite probably respond that life at any cost was better than dying. But I assumed, perhaps wrongly, that the bird had no concept of its predicament. It could not know what psychological torture it might have to endure not being able to respond to its most basic needs and desires. If it lived, it would spend the rest of its days, its years, never being able to do what its instincts demanded it should.

The end was swift and, I hope, painless. I dealt with the act knowing full well how best to conduct the task. Throughout my younger life, people would bring all manner of creatures to me, thinking that my interest in

The clown of the sea.

Winter gales whip the sea into a fury.

Oops!

Up Helly Aa. And me in a dress. Hmmm.

The burning galley at the Hillswick Up Helly Aa.

16,000 gannets breed on the cliffs of Noss.

Noss hosts some of the finest seabird colonies in the world.

The sea is almost 600 feet below. Not a place for anyone suffering from vertigo.

OK, You first! About to go over the edge with climbing expert Colin Charles.

The sandstone cliffs of Noss are sculpted by wind and weather into ledges and
cavities utilised by nesting guillemots.

The bird with the essence of wilderness in its voice: a red-throated diver.

Arctic terns. The sea swallows of Shetland.

Many quiet Shetland beaches host colonies of terns.

Filming wildlife around Shetland shores
demands a lot of leg work.

A dog otter leaving a smelly calling card, or spraint.

the natural world somehow automatically meant I knew how to fix things when they went wrong. Through reading, seeking advice, and through trial and error, I had my successes, from fledgling thrushes and poisoned gulls to infant weasels and foxes. But there were the inevitable failures, too, and I learnt the hard way how to dispatch birds quickly and with minimum suffering.

The practical act was quick and straightforward. The emotional one was enormously hard. Though I had decided to euthanise the tern, I struggled with the decision before and after doing it. I do still.

# Chapter 10

## Winter

The rest of the summer passed in a blur of activity, following otters, filming seabird colonies and hoping for other sightings of killer whales. The latter proved to be elusive, and I had to resign myself to the fact that I would only stand a chance of another orca encounter when I returned the following year. My autumn and winter were to be occupied by a long stint in Kenya filming the big cats for a feature film, with only a short trip back to the UK for the live TV series *Autumnwatch*. Shetland, and my love for the place, would have to be put on hold for the time being.

We arrived back at our house on the hill in the middle of February 2009. On this occasion we had flown into Shetland, in part to cut down the travel time, in part to avoid what we thought might be rather rough seas on a ferry crossing. As it turned out, the latter fear was unfounded, since we were greeted at Sumburgh Airport by clear skies and a gentle breeze.

On the long drive to the north of the mainland, we passed the last vestiges of snow from what had been a near complete covering of the isles a week or so before. I was a little frustrated that we had still been in Kenya when winter had graced Shetland with a white blanket. I had so wanted to see and film the islands and the wildlife here in the snow. But I consoled myself with the hope that it might snow again during our visit (it has been known to snow in Shetland in June, so February has more than a fighting chance of a good covering) and that I might be able to showcase the land in wintry splendour.

Accessing the house proved something of a challenge. Winter storms had radically changed the shape of the beach and heavy rain had swollen the little brook, or burn, into more of a torrent. This, in turn, had carved the banks of the burn to form a steep-sided ditch that could only be negotiated well down the beach where it levelled out.

During the summer months, once we had crossed the beach, we could drive the car and our gear to within twenty metres of the house, but now that the ground was sodden, we had to abandon the vehicle at the gate some three hundred metres away.

I borrowed a special all-terrain vehicle with very low weight and wheel loading to get the heaviest of our supplies and gear down the field to the cottage, but even this started to cut up the land, so the last few trips with our bags and camera cases were made on foot. By now the weather had shifted dramatically. Dark clouds had raced in from the east and a stiff wind had picked up. At one point, as I tried to wrestle our mattress through the door, a sudden gust almost lifted me, complete with bed, off my feet. It occurred to me that at least I would have had a soft landing if the wind had picked up any further.

Once inside, the mood changed dramatically. Savannah, now two and a half years old, helped me to light the fire while Marguerite got the stove going in the kitchen and prepared the beds. Darkness comes early to Shetland in the winter, the sun setting at about four in the afternoon, but the thick cloud overhead meant that it was dark even earlier than usual on this night.

By the time we had finished supper and cleared up, the house was warm and the winter dampness was already being chased from the walls. Nestled on the sofa with Savannah and Marguerite, I felt an overwhelming sense of happiness and peace. We were back, and it felt very much like home.

The following morning I was woken well before first light, which is admittedly at about seven, by gusts of wind and rain hitting our bedroom window.

'Hmmmm. Doesn't sound too nice out there,' I said to Marguerite, who had also been woken by the racket.

'What are we planning today?' she asked

'I thought we might have a look for the otters, but I don't think the weather's going to let us. Still, we can get the house and kit sorted.'

We spent the rest of the first part of the morning unpacking cameras and making sure there was nothing missing from the house inventory, and by the time there was sufficient light in the sky to see by, we were prepared to head out into the field. So that Marguerite and I could work together with the otters and other wildlife, we had organised help with Savannah with a childminder in a nearby village, a drive of some four or five miles – if we could reach her. This was a big 'if'. I donned my waterproofs and stepped out of the front door of the house to study the beach below with my binoculars. It was immediately apparent that the high tide was covering the beach completely, and that the route was impassable.

'Time for another cuppa I say,' quipped Marguerite in her usual cheery response to adversity.

We didn't manage to cross the beach until almost midday and I was acutely aware that we had very little daylight left in which to drop Savannah with the childminder, get to the spot where we hoped we would see otters, find an otter, film it, get back to pick up Savannah and get back to the house. In fact, it was impossible.

We decided instead to make this a dry run, albeit a very wet one. The rain had now turned to sleet and was being driven by a bitterly cold wind as we arrived at the east coast location where we had watched the otters a few months before. The water was being blown into a savage grey chop and, despite there being another couple of hours of daylight available, the cloud meant it was already dark enough to be dusk.

I turned to Marguerite who was in the passenger seat next to me. 'I don't think we're going to have much luck today. Let's give it half an hour, then go and pick Babba up.'

We scanned the surface of the sea, but visibility got progressively worse and we decided to pull out after only twenty minutes or so.

Savannah had been having a wonderful time with the childminder and her young daughter and was in no hurry for us to pick her up to go back to the house.

'Come on, poppet,' I urged. 'We have to get back before it gets too dark.'

'I want to play,' she answered in her most heart-melting voice.

'Sorry, my darling, we really have to go.'

I wrestled her in to her fleece and waterproofs and carried her to the car. The wind had picked up still further and the cutting cold made Savannah wince.

'Windy, Daddy. I don't like it!'

'Don't worry, sweetie, we'll be back home soon.'

By the time I had the car at the top of the hill, it was getting dark and there was a hailstorm blowing straight up the hill from the cottage.

Marguerite and I wrapped Savannah up in our spare jackets as best we could and headed down the hill for the house.

A sudden gust ripped the jacket away from Savannah's face, pelting her with hail.

'Ouch, Daddy, it's raining stones!'

Never was it more eloquently put.

The heinous conditions didn't change the following day. Nor the one after that. I began to worry that the event I had hoped to witness at this time of year might be cancelled. For once this did not involve the wildlife of Shetland – although, on reflection, perhaps it did!

Up Helly Aa is a festival held throughout the isles from January to mid-March. It started life some hundred and fifty years ago when teams of young men, in desperate need of amusement and diversion in the midst of the darkness and cold of winter, ran through the villages and towns in varying states of inebriation. They apparently accompanied their high spirits with burning barrels of tar. Local authorities took exception to the increasingly dangerous nature of the revelry, and decided to formalise the celebrations, hence Up Helly Aa was properly born. Shetland has a strong and tangible Norse heritage and, to echo this, as the celebrations became more formal and structured, they took on a distinctly Viking theme. The present-day celebrations are led by Jarl squads: teams of men (and sometimes women) dressed in the most elaborate Viking regalia. The members of these teams prepare a good year in advance of their turn to lead the festivities; all the men growing suitably shaggy beards and everyone making and investing in outfits of the most astonishing level of quality and detail. The Jarl squad, headed up by the Guizer Jarl (head Viking), leads a procession through town, each man and woman holding a flaming torch and pulling a specially built Viking galley on a trailer. These ships are often huge, and beautifully crafted by the squads. Traditional songs are sung and, climactically, the flaming torches are thrown on to the galley to set it ablaze.

This is what I had read about and this is what I wanted to witness. What I did not realise was that this was just a part of the exercise – a very important part of course; but it turned out that there was a lot more to Up Helly Aa than I had ever imagined.

A day or so before the event in my local community in Northmarine was due to take place, I was contacted by

Helen Moncrieff (she of the leg-wrestling fame) to say that I had been invited to join a squad. I was astonished and very honoured and imagined myself dressed in full Viking battle gear, clutching a flaming torch and roaring at the sky.

On the night, which as it turned out was relatively calm and only a little drizzly, I found myself wearing a nylon dress and a blonde wig.

Let me explain.

Having managed to get away from the cottage (and book into a hotel on the mainland for the night to ensure we would all be able to return to a bed once the festival was over), I had driven with Marguerite and Savannah to a remote cafe with a caravan site where we were to meet with the rest of the squads and prepare for the evening.

We had visited this cafe once or twice before in the summer and enjoyed delicious food and spectacular views over the bay below. Our fellow customers then had been folk who'd been camping or staying in their caravans on site. This evening, the clientele were somewhat – how shall I put it – different. As I stepped through the door, I was greeted by several young women dressed as rather rotund, scruffy men, right down to beards drawn on to their faces with eyeliner. After a brief chat I discovered they were in fact supposed to be Trows, which is the Shetland equivalent of a mischievous goblin. Right then.

I then noticed Michael Jackson waiting at the counter for a bowl of soup and Elton John sitting at a table with other 'A' list celebrities sipping beers from cans. I recognised Elton John as Jonathan, the chap with whom I had been shearing sheep in the summer.

'Simon, over here. Come on over,' Elton shouted, beckoning me to join his table.

'Aye, aye Simon. Set you down. What'll you have? Help yersel.' Jonathan gestured to a stack of lagers in the middle of the table.

It was clear now that there was more than one squad on the night. Indeed, there were many, but only one was the Jarl squad dressed as Vikings. The rest were teams of Shetlanders who registered to take part in Up Helly Aa and who prepared costumes and performances of their own. The form for the evening was for the Jarl squad to lead a march from the small village of Hillswick, down the road to the sea, followed by the galley and a train of other people in squads, plus many more who lined the street to watch the proceedings. Once the formal singing and boat-burning had been satisfactorily executed, the whole crowd moved to the nearby village halls, where food and drink were to hand. Then, one by one, each squad visited and did a performance. It is traditional that, with the exception of the Vikings who sing a formal series of ballads that have been handed down over the years, the squads have an act prepared – which is often a satire of a local issue, figure or event. My squad had prepared a show that involved various well-known people admiring an art exhibition, and, one by one, being kidnapped by the Trows. The finale was a rescue conducted by one of the team. Apparently there had been an exhibition of local art in a nearby hall in the summer and this was a reference to it. I think. To be absolutely honest, I had no idea what political satire our act was supposed to convey, and still don't. I was just enjoying being part of it. After some debate it was decided that I should come as Kate Humble, my fellow presenter from the live TV series *Springwatch*. I was game, but singularly ill prepared. I was still wearing my fleece and jeans and, though Kate wears the very same most of the time on screen, I did not think anyone would spot that I was in costume. One of the chaps at the table volunteered his help.

'Come wi me. I bide joost doon da rod at Eshaness. I hae somethin du can use.'

I left Marguerite and Savannah enjoying their supper and hopped in my friend's car. After a short drive we pulled in through the gate of his property and up to his house.

'Dunna mind da dog. He'll no hcrm dee.'

He opened the front door and I found myself face to face with one of the biggest Great Danes I had ever seen in my life. I was glad to have been forewarned.

I greeted the dog and we followed on through the kitchen to a storeroom. After a bit of rummaging, my friend appeared clutching what looked like a dead cat in one hand and a tea towel in the other.

'There y'are. That'll do dee,' he said, handing me a dark blue nylon dress with a bold white print, and a matted long blonde wig.

It struck me as a bit odd that he might have a dress and wig in his size to hand, but accepted the outfit with thanks, and later realised that a good percentage of the population is prepared for last-minute silly costume events, such is the nature of self-made fun in the isles.

Suitably attired, we returned to the cafe and I entered feeling more than a little ridiculous. Though I received a few funny looks as I walked amongst the Trows and back to Elton John's table, I began to feel very much a part of the fun.

'Hello Daddy,' piped Savannah, after looking at me quizzically for a few seconds. 'Why are you wearing that?'

I was shocked and a little offended that she had recognised me so quickly.

'Very good question, my darling. I'm not entirely sure myself.'

Now ready, we all got into our respective vehicles and headed for the centre of Hillswick town. The Vikings were in position and various helpers and stewards were handing out thin fence posts, their tips wrapped in hessian sacking and dipped in a flammable liquid.

And then we were off. Ranks of people, in the most eclectic mix of costume, walked three or four abreast, brandishing their flaming torches and from time to time yelling 'Raaaar!' or 'Aaaaargh!' or other such suitably Viking-like utterances. After a little while, I began to feel less self-conscious about my attire, and joined in with the occasional 'Yaaaaaargh!'

I still had no idea what I was doing but, whatever it was, it was fun, and that was the point really. The warmth of community, the energy to create an event that was not to boost the tourist trade or get headlines but to have a good time together. It was a face of Shetland I had seen before in simple hospitality and disarming friendship. It was another reason I had grown to love it even more.

By the time we had reached the water's edge I had fully joined in the spirit of the proceedings and was sporting a wide grin. The galley, over which so much time and care had been lavished, was pushed off its trailer into the sea and, led by the Vikings, we each of us threw our torches into its hull. It drifted off into the darkness; a blazing dragon on a black sea.

Once it had been swallowed by the inky waters, we headed for the village hall, where there was much chat, singing, eating and drinking. It was getting late for Savannah, but Marguerite had kindly volunteered to take her back to the hotel in Brae and stay with her there, awaiting my return.

'Be careful,' she whispered into my ear just before leaving. 'Don't drink too much.' With that she and Savannah gave me a hug and left me to my squad.

The rest of the evening was spent travelling over the whole of the north section of the mainland in a minibus captained by our nominated and, of course, entirely sober driver. This task felt like the short straw early on in the evening, but as time went on I began to see the wisdom in it.

We stopped at each village hall, piled out of the van, joined other squads and performed our little set piece. Our Trow kidnap extravaganza was acted out with ever greater conviction as, conversely, the plot grew progressively thinner, but it drew warm applause from the discerning public in each of the halls. Post-performance I chatted with everyone I met, some in full costume, most along to enjoy the festivities. Every hall had an impressive spread of food which seemed to be handed out freely, and drink was dispensed by each of the squads from temporary bars.

By the time we had reached North Roe village hall I was warm with friendship of my fellow man and the occasional tot of malt whisky. I danced, chatted, ate and drank; rarely had I felt more relaxed and unselfconscious in new company, despite still sporting a wig and a nylon dress. This evening was for the people, by the people of Shetland, and we were all comfortable in our tribe, one that I had gate-crashed but had been warmly welcomed into.

The party ended as light came back to the sky, and I was among the last of the squad to be dropped off by our valiant driver.

I crept into the hotel and into bed next to Marguerite, who stirred a little, smiled at me and asked what time it was.

'About eight I think. I'm not sure. I'm a wee bit tired.' With that I fell into a deep, happy sleep.

The respite in the weather that allowed for the Up Helly Aa celebrations was short-lived. Wind and rain made the short days nothing more than a brief, protracted dusk, and opportunities to film wildlife were few and far between. We spent some time trying to film mountain hares in the heather moors near the east coast, but even this relatively simple task took us three attempts due to the savage wind speeds vibrating the camera and telephoto lenses. We saw otters on a couple of occasions, but each time the light was so poor that filming them was a no-hoper. But the difficulties we faced trying to film wildlife were exacerbated tenfold by the problems we had getting to and from our house on the hill. The continued rain cut the banks of the burn ever deeper, and a spell of particularly high winds and tides pushed the sea up the beach, making it impassable for many hours of the day. I would wake in the dark and look out only to find that I would have to wait two or three hours to try and get out to the road and drive to my otter location. I decided to concentrate efforts on watching the otters on our doorstep, but even this tactic was scuppered by the weather. I had one halcyon dawn, with lemon light irradiating the far shore and a stillness so profound that I could literally have heard a pin drop. I waited on the bay below the house in an area littered with otter sign, optimistic that I would get a glimpse of my wild neighbour. By mid-morning, my hopes were driven away by a sudden and violent shift in the weather again. I hunched into a storm-force wind and icy rain for an hour before giving up and heading back up the hill to the house.

At least the conditions gave me time to be with Savannah, and we spent hours drawing and reading by the fire. Had I been based at the house full time, perhaps working the land and using supplies that I had stored from the summer, I could see the appeal of this little cocoon on the hill; door bolted against the elements, peat burning in the fire. Life here in times gone by would have been tough, but it would have had its simple pleasures. I adored having time to spend with my daughter and Marguerite together, but meanwhile my attempts to film the island's wildlife were being thwarted by the wind and tide. My plans were starting to unravel and it frustrated me.

\*

One mission that simply had to be conducted in the early part of the year involved the sea cliffs of Noss. I had an ambition to put a remote camera close to a gannet's nest, and the only way I could access their breeding cliffs without undue disturbance was before they had taken up residence in the spring. We had no TV at the house, but could just manage a slow, mobile Internet connection on which we could access weather reports; these showed day after day of isobars so close together they blended into one. A gap of twenty-four hours of calmer weather looked possible in the middle of the week, and we prepared to make the most of it.

A climbing team was flown up from England. Together with Martin the producer, who is a very accomplished climber, I and the rest of the team set off bright and early on what looked to be a very promising morning to meet the boatmen in Lerwick harbour. As we loaded the gear on to the boat, I was a little disconcerted to see a number of stout metal crosses with sharpened ends in the climbers' kit.

'Not planning any burials?' I quipped, with a hint of concern in my voice.

'Just making sure we're ready for anything,' answered Colin, the head climber. 'You never know, there could be a vampire among us!'

It was explained to me that the stakes were to be our rope anchor points, hammered into the soil on the cliff top. I hoped that they wouldn't end up serving an ironic double purpose.

Once we had made the sea journey to Noss, we unloaded

the ropes, camera kit, metal stakes and assorted climbing kit on to the little rock jetty, and from there into the trailer of the shepherd's quad. This would speed up the movement of gear to the cliffs in the east, but most of the team still had to walk the mile or so across the island, eating into precious daylight hours. Marguerite was to stay on board the boat and film the action from below. Almost six hundred feet below.

I waved farewell to Marguerite as she and the boat crew set off to the far side of Noss; after a sweat-inducing walk, we reached the top of the gannet cliffs. There were already many birds flying to and fro along the cliff face, but none yet had started to build nest platforms and the majority had still to arrive to take up residence on their traditional nesting ledges. Colin and his climbing assistant carefully rigged the ropes and safety lines, whilst I helped to prepare the camera kit and hammer the stakes into the ground. I took special care in this task, for obvious reasons. Satisfied that we could hang an elephant off the anchor points should we so wish, I checked the cliffs below for likely nest ledges. There were few points where I could get a good view, but I thought I could see a good ledge some thirty or forty feet below us, and this would be our target.

Harness on and roped in, with cameras fitted to our climbing helmets and a bag full of tools and more camera gear, Colin and I prepared to abseil down the cliff. Martin was to abseil too, a little further along the cliff, and film us at work, while Marguerite recorded events from below, and our cameraman/director Nick would cover events from the top. As I prepared to push my weight against the rope and swing my body over the drop, I felt a flicker of unease in my belly. I am quite used to heights and have done a fair bit of work on ropes, but I wouldn't describe myself as a knowledgeable or experienced climber. I have never been climbing as a recreation and all my rope-access knowledge comes from having to use safety lines in trees or on precipitous cliff faces when trying to film wildlife. This was new to me. Pushing myself out over a three-hundred-metre sheer drop was counterintuitive. I had absolute faith in the gear, my guide and climb leader and, perhaps most importantly, the metal stakes upon which our lives depended, but it's hard not to contemplate the 'what if' scenario as you put your faith and life into the hands of all these variables. I had no need, nor time, to be concerned, though. After a bit of a scrabble to get over the edge we were soon abseiling down the cliff, seeing it – for the first time – as the gannets and fulmars that nest here do. The view was spectacular. Hundreds of birds passed below and around us, striking white against the slaty sea. From time to time, a fulmar would pass within a metre or so of us, stiff wings twitching to adjust to the ever-shifting airflow, dark eyes staring into our own.

'Let's take a moment,' suggested Colin. He was the consummate climber: relaxed, confident, and utterly in love with what he did.

'Beautiful, isn't it?' he said, looking out across the sea below. I had been concentrating hard on my footholds, ropes and descending gear, and had not taken the time to really appreciate the astonishing privilege of what we were doing.

'Stunning,' I answered, and for a moment allowed my imagination and spirit to fly with the birds around me.

We continued our descent a few more metres before we came to the ledge. It had clearly been the site of at least two gannet nests the year before, but all that was left of the nest structures was a brown, slimy patch of composted grass and guano.

'It looks perfect,' I said, turning to Colin who was beginning to pull the tool kit from his back. 'Let's try to get the two cameras in: one looking across the cliff; the other looking down at the nest.'

We had with us a powerful drill, resin, and metal rods that would provide the camera mounts. We would not be able to access the ledge once the birds were in residence, so everything we did now had to last throughout the year.

Drilling the holes in the sandstone rock face was tougher than I had predicted, taking much longer than planned. Getting the resin glue out of the glue gun proved to be even harder, either because it was so cold or I had just lost my punch. Either way, we were on the cliff for a good hour before the job was done. With the two mini cameras finally in position, we knew we had to get back to the top as fast as possible. The boat did not want to be messing around in the dark getting us off the island, particularly with changeable weather in prospect.

By the time Colin and I came back up the ropes and were on the cliff top, there was a distinct hint of dusk settling into the sky. We still had to de-rig the ropes, and get back across the island to the quay in the west, and rapidly closing evening was now threatening to make the whole exercise considerably more tricky than we'd hoped. By the time we made it to the quay, hot and sweating from the fast walk back, the boatmen had already loaded the kit from the shepherd's trailer on board and were urging us to join them quickly.

'There's a storm on the way. We have to be out of here before dark, lads. Let's go!'

We had achieved the first stage of our goal, but only just. It served to illustrate once again how tricky it was to get things done at this latitude in winter – even late winter, as this was. Now back with Marguerite, we thanked everyone for their sterling efforts, and made a dash for home, picking up Savannah from the childminder on the way.

By the time we reached the beach below our house, the weather had turned again and we battled another icy shower to get to our front door. I was beginning to realise that, if we wanted to have regular close contact with the wildlife of Shetland, then I had made an error of judgement in choosing this house as our base. Certainly, it was in a beautiful setting, and we were indeed surrounded by wild creatures. But filming on the doorstep had proven to be tricky and getting in and out of the house was unpredictable. Regretfully, Marguerite and I came to the conclusion that we would have to relocate when we returned to Shetland in the spring. In this way, every hour of the day could be spent with the wildlife, instead of managing domestic logistics.

# Chapter 11

## Hope Springs Eternal

Just before we were due to leave the isles for a few weeks, I received news that a young otter had been found, abandoned and injured, and taken into care by Jan and Pete Bevington. They run a wildlife sanctuary in Hillswick, in the northwest of the island, specialising in the care of marine mammals, especially seals and otters. They had had many success stories over the years, and worked tirelessly to relieve the suffering of unfortunate creatures that had fallen foul of bad weather, illness or man's destructive ways, intentional or otherwise.

I met with Jan at her house, which doubles as the sanctuary, on another windy wet day. She was a gently spoken, private woman, who oozed dedication, love and commitment to her cause. Kirikoo, as the little otter had been named by one of Jan's young relatives, was no more than a couple of months old when she first came into Jan's care. The otter had been seen wandering alone in the back garden of a house on the island of Bressay, calling for its mother. The homeowner had kept an eye on it, but it was clear that it was not going to be reunited after a couple of days, and if any more time went by with no food it would certainly die. Unfortunately, the decision to bring it into care was forced by the homeowner's dog, a Labrador, that gently tried to carry the little scrap into the house. The otter had struggled in the dog's soft jaws, and damaged its own back as a result. Now it was paralysed from the hips down, dragging its hind legs and tail as it pulled its weight along with its forefeet. Its future was far from certain.

Though Jan had been doing everything in her power to help the cub, dedicating many hours of every day to nurturing it back to good health, she was also a pragmatist and realised that life for an otter that couldn't swim, and was therefore committed to a future in captivity, was no life at all. That said, she was an optimist too, and continued to work hard to encourage Kirikoo to use her hindquarters. Since the cub had arrived at the sanctuary, there had been signs of improvement. Jan and Pete had been using slices of fresh fish to tempt the otter to reach up and use its back legs and, from time to time, it had done so. It seemed as though any damage done during the accident with the dog was nerve-based and might not be permanent. This was reason enough for Jan's optimism to blossom, and she had thrown herself wholeheartedly into the task of re-educating Kirikoo to use her legs again.

When I visited, I was taken to meet Kirikoo in her indoor enclosure, and at first I was dismayed by what I saw. She had no problem whatsoever with her forefeet, powerfully trotting all over the floor of the pen. But her hindquarters and tail dragged uselessly behind.

But once a little fish was introduced to the scene, things started to change. At first one, then the other hind foot was pulled up into a walking position, and then the cub stretched high to reach the meal from Jan's fingers. It looked like a teasing torture, but it was clear that this was the only way Kirikoo would bother to use her whole body. With enough of this kind of treatment, she might regain full use of her mobility and be able to be released to the wild. Tough love at its very best.

I was hugely impressed by Jan and Pete's approach. It was sympathetic and humane, and at the same time realistic. But the driving force behind their commitment was a natural empathy with the plight of wild spirits that had fallen on hard times.

I thanked Jan for including me in her work, albeit briefly, and left vowing to return in the spring to see how Kirikoo was progressing.

The winter trip to the isles had been essential for the preparation of certain film projects that I hoped would blossom in the spring, but it had been generally frustrating too. We never did get any more snow, only wind and rain, and enough of that to last the rest of the year. We had found it very difficult to film what wildlife there was in the isles, too – because of the weather, of course, but also because of our compromised position in our charming but rather too remote cottage.

I made a careful check of alternative properties before we left the isles, and settled on a spot where road access was good, as was proximity to first-class otter habitat. Our return in a few weeks' time would not be dominated by the tide in quite the same way.

Shetland comes alive in the early spring. The length of

the day races towards summer's endless light at astonishing speed, and by April the isles are fizzing with natural excitement. Our return was timed to coincide with the arrival of the summer migrants to the isles, and the beginning of the seabird breeding season. I hoped that our remote cameras in the gannet colony would be revealing a new and intimate view of their family life, and that we would be able to feature some of the myriad birds that flock to Shetland to breed. Of course, the chance to catch up properly with otters was high on the agenda too but, to kick off, there was another facet of human life on the isles that beckoned.

Shetland has a reputation for creating fine folk music, and the musicians that play it. A casual chat to a gathering virtually anywhere on the isles will almost invariably reveal a couple of fiddle, guitar or accordion players, as well as a piano tickler or two. In the past I had seen folk – in their vehicles on the ferries that link the isles – while away the time on the sea by playing the whistle, or even a fiddle, in the cab of their van. Music and Shetland were inextricably linked. And the Shetland Folk Festival was an event held in April where fine exponents of their musical art could showcase their skills. In its twenty-nine-year existence it had developed a sufficient reputation to attract artists from around the world, and this year performers from Canada, Scandinavia and the Baltics were in the line-up. Seeing at least some of the sets seemed a fitting reconnection to the energy of Shetland life. As it turned out, I had the honour of opening the proceedings and introducing a medley from some of the fine musicians who would be playing over the weekend. I was concerned

Savannah might be overawed by the loud music and raucous applause, but not a bit of it. The moment the music started she was jigging up and down and clapping with the best of them, a broad grin fixed permanently to her face.

The following evening, having moved our gear into our new rented house on the east side of the mainland, we attended an impromptu concert in Lerwick, featuring some of the most talented musicians I had seen for years. I recognised faces that I had passed by in town, but now they were the stars of the show, whipping up a storm with their folky strains. In the next room, a band based in Edinburgh produced a rich fusion of rock and world music, and everywhere people danced and smiled. Once again, I was reminded of the desire and energy in Shetland to have a good time and to get along with your fellow man. Heart-warming stuff.

With a good fix of community spirit under our belts, we were able to settle into the main objective and go in search of wild creatures. A couple of days spent at our original otter location revealed that the mother and large cub had gone their separate ways, and none had been born recently to take their place. I wanted to follow otter family life, and the location of our next house was ideally placed for the task. The voe that stretched to the north in front of the cottage was ideal otter habitat and, furthermore, perfect topographically for filming them. Even better, John Campbell had watched the otters here for years, and kindly offered to accompany me and Marguerite to help us get a feel for the land and to point out where the holts, drinking spots and favourite sleeping rocks were along the coastline.

It took no more than a few minutes' walking along the coastline, a couple of miles from our house, to realise just how marvellous a spot this was for filming otters. Everywhere I looked there was sign of spraint, and the low peat banks made it possible to scan the waters without being seen. A steep hill offered the perfect vantage point for a broad view of the territory, but the jewel in the crown was the lagoon. This wide stretch of brackish water was protected from the worst of the weather from almost any direction by the hills, was not overlooked by any house or road, however distant, and offered the otters in the neighbourhood a wonderful feeding and resting ground. On our first morning out, we picked up the swimming form of an otter on the lagoon, or 'pond', as John called it, within half an hour of arriving.

'I reckon that's the young male,' John whispered. 'The mum here has three cubs, two girls and a boy. I think that's her son. They're all big now, but still together a lot of the time. I'm surprised he's on his own.'

My heart sank a little at this news. I was delighted to see an otter, of course, but I had hoped to follow a young family. The suggestion was that this group of otters would be splitting up in the near future, and I was too late to see them as a tightly knit family unit.

As I watched and filmed the young male, a new thought dawned. What if the separation were not yet complete? I might be lucky enough to witness and film this testing period in the lives of the cubs. It was too much to hope for, but the prospect nourished my enthusiasm. I had in the past only ever seen families together, or already separated. Witnessing the ephemeral period when the adult female turns from being a nurturing mother to a short-tempered stranger must be very confusing for the cubs, and an event worth charting on film.

As I mulled this over, the otter on the lagoon started calling.

John leant forward and studied the scene through his binoculars. 'He must have spotted his mum,' he murmured as he scoured the water for signs of a new arrival. 'Here she comes, down the burn from the holt.'

The adult female paused on the brilliant green lawn of salt-hardy grass at the fringe of the lagoon and delivered her smelly calling card on a pile of peat. She then entered the water with seamless grace and swam to where her well-grown cub was whistling wildly and paddling fast to join her. As they came together in the water, their noses met briefly, and the cub, as big as his mum and rather more chunky in build, tried in vain to get her to join in a bout of wrestling. His mother wasn't hostile to her cub, but she wasn't about to play, either, when finding a meal was the more pressing duty of the day.

The pair swam out to the centre of the lagoon and, as I filmed their progress, were joined by a third otter, which I took to be one of the female cubs.

'What an incredible place John. Three otters in less than an hour. Amazing!'

'I don't know why I'm showing you all my favourite otter-watching spots,' John quipped. 'I must be going soft.'

We followed the three with camera and binoculars as they dived and caught small fish, each otter obviously well able to look after itself on the fishing front, but still keen to come together for a groom and cuddle from time to time.

'Where do you think the other female cub is?' I asked.

'Probably sleeping off a good meal. They're all pretty much independent now. Just sticking close to mum for comfort.'

We continued to follow the family as they swam up to and broached the shingle bar that acted as a barrier between the lagoon and the open sea of the voe. Running to catch up, we rounded the shingle and caught sight of the family about a hundred metres off shore.

The rest of the afternoon was spent keeping track of them until they eventually all retreated to a holt in a peat bank towards the open sea.

'Absolutely gorgeous, John, thank you. I reckon if I put the hours in, I may see the split.'

John answered in his usual generous and affable way. 'Not a problem. Any time you want a bit of help and company, just give me a bell.'

The following day, I decided to explore the area around our new living quarters more fully. Having established that I had relatively easy access to otters, I wanted to record some of the bustle of life that spring brings to the isles, and a quick check of the ground below the house revealed two oystercatcher nests, both with eggs. Having worked with oiks when making *Springwatch* a couple of years earlier, I knew that, though common, they could be fascinating to watch, and if I spent a bit of time I might be able to record a fun sequence with them. One of the nests was sited on the edge of a tightly grazed field that was holding a herd of lambing sheep. It rang echoes from the past, convincing me this was the spot where I should concentrate my efforts.

At first glance, it seems curious that any ground-nesting bird should choose to risk its clutch of eggs by laying them in a field occupied by the owners of hundreds of frolicking hooves. But oystercatchers may sometimes decide to nest close to human settlements because their natural predators, such as skuas and gulls, are less likely to patrol the skies there. These birds must assess the risk of having their eggs crushed accidentally against that of predation, and plump for the woolly threat over the feathered one. At least they can effectively dissuade the lambs from coming too close with a well-placed peck.

With the action taking place so close to home, this was also a chance for a certain young apprentice to cut her teeth in wildlife camera work. Savannah had already travelled with us on several occasions whilst we were working in Kenya, and this was her third stay in Shetland. In the past she had been too young to want to sit in a hide and watch a bird for any longer than a couple of minutes. Now, at almost three, I thought she might be ready for a more in-depth exposure.

Soon after finding the oystercatcher nest, I had placed one of my mini remote cameras, camouflaged with rocks, close to its edge on the ground in the hope of getting a low, wide view of the activity. I ran the cable from the camera twenty metres through the grass and planned to return later with a hide and my small, willing assistant to record the action.

Back at the house, to help Savannah get to grips with what we were about to film at the nest, I used another little camera to illustrate the basic principles. We focused it on one of her cuddly toys, and she learned how to record an image of what appeared to be a giant Winnie the Pooh by operating the recording deck. She handled this phase of the operation with skill and precision, only briefly and accidentally standing on the camera once she'd had enough of the lesson and wanted her toy back.

With her operator skills finely honed it was time to prepare her for the mission ahead.

'Do you know what those birds are down at the bottom of the field?' I asked, pointing out a nearby oystercatcher that was feeding whilst its mate incubated the eggs.

'Oystercatcher,' came the clear reply.

I glowed with pride. 'That's right, my darling, and they have a long red nose, don't they?'

She thought for a moment. 'I have a tiny nose.'

She was well on the way to being a top field-craft expert.

Together, we organised and bagged all the kit and set off down the field towards the nest, me carrying cameras, tripod, hide and rucksack full of assorted batteries and tapes, Savannah with her Winnie the Pooh cuddly toy. At one point she rather lost focus, heading off in the direction of the sea whilst singing the elephant marching song from *The Jungle Book*, but, after a gentle reminder, was right back on track.

The next phase of her training was a lesson in how to put up a portable hide, or — as it turned out — how *not* to.

I explained the basic principles of remaining hidden from the nest so that we didn't put the mummy birds or the daddy bird off the eggs otherwise they would get cold and sick, and she nodded sagely at the possible repercussions of too much disturbance.

And so on to the lesson. I thought I would impress her by using a large, two-man structure that unfolded instantly like a giant umbrella. At least it did if you knew what you were doing. I'd like to pretend that the hide was poorly packed or that it was the first time I had tried to erect it, but the fact is I had done it many times before, and the last person who had packed it away was me. The law of 'don't try to show off to your daughter, you'll just look like an idiot' kicked in, and I began a wrestling match with the hide that was clearly one-sided, the hide winning from the start.

From time to time Savannah offered words of encouragement, like, 'Is it ready, Daddy?' and 'Can we go yet?', all of which were reasonable under the circumstances. At one point I fell inside the flailing legs and roof of the hide and heard a plaintive voice ask, 'Can I come in now?'

Eventually, though, I managed to punch the structure into its proper shape and prepare for the next phase of the apprenticeship: moving the hide in. There are several different approaches one can take when introducing a hide to a ground-nesting bird. The first is by building a structure gradually over a number of days so that a bird gets used to the new form in its territory. Another technique is to erect a hide at a distance and to move it closer to the nest bit by bit.

The method I decided would be most enlightening for Savannah was walking in. The hide in question, now properly erected, was rigid and freestanding. This meant we could get inside, lift it up and walk with it, and together we began our curious waddle across the field to get the hide to within twenty metres of the nest. At one point I caught a glimpse through the window of a couple of sheep that were clearly somewhat perplexed by this moving bush complete with four legs; the two at the front rather smaller than the rear pair.

Once we reached the point where I had earlier placed the ends of the remote camera cables, we settled the hide down on the ground and pulled back one of the flaps that cover the small windows to check the view. We were able to see the oystercatcher still sitting on its nest, looking a little confused but otherwise unfazed by our arrival. Most creatures are pretty brave when faced with an entirely unknown object. The hide 'walking' to within twenty metres did not compute as a danger, but if we had walked in brazenly and unhidden, the bird would have been off the nest in a flash.

I got the recording deck and monitor out of my rucksack and Savannah, with her operator skills having been honed a little earlier on Pooh, prepared to fire the whole thing up. As an image flickered on to the screen she leant in to study her results.

'There's an oystercatcher,' she whispered, eyes wide with concentration and amazement.

The view afforded by the remote camera was intimate

and fun, the long red beak of the oik reaching almost to the lens, making it look much longer than it was.

'He has a very long nose, Daddy.'

We watched the nest on the screen together, waiting for any change in the sitting bird's behaviour, with Savannah pressing the record button to capture it on tape. Once or twice a lamb came too close for the oystercatcher's comfort, and received a firm peck on the head, all on camera. Savannah's first official job as camera assistant had been a complete success.

As long as the weather held fair, I concentrated on filming the wildlife around our new home. In addition to the otters and oystercatchers, a few red-throated divers were spending most of their day on the voe. They would soon be settling to nest on the borders and islands of remote hill lochs, but for now much of their time was being spent resting on the open water near the house. From time to time their haunting voices rose up from the far side of the bay, and bounced off the surrounding hillsides. The natural music of Shetland was finding its voice now. Blackbird song filled the air around the house, and the warbling fluty calls of curlew displaying over the nearby moorland added plaintive tones to the mix.

Early spring can be changeable, though, and it was inevitable the conditions would shift during our stay. A strong wind blew in from the west, making it very difficult to hold a camera steady in our usual haunts. John Campbell came to the rescue once more with an otter-watching spot he often used when the wind picked up. A ruined croft provided shelter and overlooked a wide bay with a small island just off shore. The island was often used by otters as a resting place and, tucked in the lee of the wind, I could scan the scene without the telephoto lens being blown about too severely.

I decided that even though these were not otters I had followed up to now, it was better to make the most of what at least was dry – if windy – weather, and planned to meet John at the spot.

'Morning, John. Blowing a bit of a hooligan this morning,' I shouted above the wind as we greeted each other in the small car park.

'Not a worry; we'll be nicely out of it when we get to the croft.'

John was right, of course. By the time we reached the tumbledown ruins of the old farmhouse and were tucked low behind one of its walls, barely a breath of wind stirred our hiding place. By contrast, the sea before us was being whipped into a choppy mass of grey and white peaks, breaking into a horizontal spray against the rocks of the island.

'It's not going to be easy to spot an otter in this,' I suggested.

'Don't worry, we'll pick them up when they come on to the island,' John said cheerily. 'Actually, take a look in the middle right now.'

I studied the sparse vegetation through my binoculars and saw what John was talking about. Bang in the centre of the greenery, tucked out of the wind behind a rock, was the russet-brown flank of a sleeping otter.

'Nice one, John. You've done it again mate,' I said with a smile.

I settled to watch how things would develop, delighted to be able to spend time in the company of a wild otter despite the gale. After a short while, the sleeping animal stirred, lifted its head and scratched its chin and, through the camera viewfinder, I noticed it was not alone. A second otter was curled up beside the first; this was almost certainly a mother with her large cub. Despite the high wind, the morning was getting ever more promising; the chances of the two grooming each other or perhaps having a bit of a wrestle were high if we waited patiently. As it turned out, neither occurred, due to the arrival of a third, larger otter on to the island, wet from a bout of fishing. After close scrutiny, both John and I agreed this was an adult male. The plot thickened. Was this chap simply doing the rounds of his territory? He would probably be given short shrift by the mother otter if he tried to get too close to her cub, and I prepared to film the face-off.

The dog otter sniffed the rocks below the resting pair, added his own scented mark, and trotted further up the island to where they lay. As he neared them he slowed and lowered his head. The wind was too strong to pick up much of the sound they were making, but I could see that the female had noticed his approach and she too had her head lowered and mouth slightly agape. The high, reedy, wavering call of an excited otter drifted over the water to where we crouched.

'I don't think she's too chuffed to see him, John,' I mumbled, with my eye to the eyepiece of the camera.

The dog approached the now alert mother and her large cub slowly, and started to sniff the vegetation close by.

He then strode purposefully up to the female and their noses met. The cub, clearly confused and upset, was squirming behind his mum, and finally his nerve broke and he turned and trotted away up the slope. The dog showed not a flicker of interest in the cub but instead stayed focused on the female. In the past, when I had seen encounters between adult females with their cubs and adult males, the reception had usually been hostile, the mum telling the male to clear off. This was different. The female started to roll on her back and twist in a provocative fashion in the grass. This encouraged the male to sniff her more closely and the pair began to wrestle gently on their sides. They then broke apart and started to chase like youngsters, to and fro on top of the island.

I thought perhaps I had become confused by the fast-moving action and it was the mother with her cub now chasing, but a check with John confirmed that the cub was still crouching in the grass and watching its mother playing with the male. There was a very strong chance that this was his father, though male otters have little to do with raising the family. The fact that the adult female was not hostile to the dog suggested that she was thinking about starting a new family, though this was unusual given that she still had a cub in tow.

The games of chase led the pair into the sea, where they porpoised and rolled in the choppy surf. Despite the heavy swell and wind-whipped spume, the otters used the water as a falcon uses the air; they were faultlessly graceful, powerful and unconsciously beautiful.

Once or twice, the male held the female in an embrace,

and for a moment I thought that I might be about to witness the rare moment of mating, but the cuddle broke off as swiftly as it started. This young lady was certainly flirtatious, but not quite ready to commit just yet.

My concentration on the courting otters was suddenly broken by a high-pitched, familiar call.

'Arctic terns,' I blurted. 'They're back! Spring has officially sprung.'

Coming in from the west, a low-flying squadron of about twenty birds powered its way into the wind: paper-light pointed wings cutting the air. As they neared the shore they called and rose higher into the air, as though the sight of their final destination after such a gargantuan journey from the southern hemisphere warranted celebration. I felt my spirits lift with them. They were the embodiment of hope and new life, of endeavour and achievement, and my thoughts were lost for a moment in their world, sharing their apparent joy. More flocks poured in from the sea, their arrival every bit as uplifting as the first swallows in the south. Soon they would crowd into their colonies and begin the season's challenging duties of raising families, but in this brief window they seemed to be concerned with nothing more than the achievement of completing their marathon for another season.

Witnessing the first arrival of a spring migrant, or the departure of a swallow or other traveller in the autumn from a southern coastal headland, is, for me, very moving. These little bundles of flesh, feather and bone throw themselves into a hostile and challenging future with absolute confidence and commitment. They do not hesitate; they do not appear to plan or prepare in any way other than feeding well before they make the leap; but, nonetheless, they achieve journeys that to my eyes are nothing short of miraculous. It may sound mawkish, but watching the terns arriving back in Shetland, after the long dark days of winter in the north, was truly inspirational. If ever I felt tired or my enthusiasm wavered, I could conjure up an image of their optimism, their blind trust in the future, and use it as a model of hope.

As the flocks of terns flickered over the turquoise sea into the distance, I directed my attention back to the otters once more. The high spirits of the pair had waned a little, the male in all likelihood deciding that if the moment wasn't quite right, then he would have to visit another day soon when the female was more compliant. Both had returned to the island and were drying off and grooming their fine fur in the wind and sun. The cub was still keeping its distance, but gradually sneaking closer to its mum. She met him halfway, the two stopping to groom each other's back and shoulders. The dog had now lost interest entirely and slipped back into the water, almost immediately coming up with a butterfish and chomping it as he floated on the bouncing surface. I marvelled at how relaxed he was in a sea state that would make me think twice about taking a swim. After a further fifteen minutes, all the otters were in the water and going their separate ways. For a day that could very easily have been a complete wipe-out due to the high wind, things hadn't turned out too badly, really.

# Chapter 12

## At Home with the Gannets

The high wind persisted and was joined by occasional downpours the following day, reason enough to check on the little otter, Kirikoo, that was being cared for at the Hillswick Wildlife Sanctuary.

Jan invited me in for a coffee and a catch-up on the cub's progress since I had last seen her a month or so ago.

'I'm not happy, Simon,' Jan said sombrely. 'She just isn't making progress like I'd hoped she would.'

I learned that Jan had sought advice from all quarters and eventually been directed to a chap who specialised in animal physiotherapy. In addition to the incentive-led strategy that she had been using to get Kirikoo to use her hind legs, she had started a dedicated and regular regime of direct manipulation of her hindquarters. I joined Jan and Pete to take a look for myself at the little otter, and was dismayed by what I saw. Though perfectly happy looking, she was dragging her back legs as much as – if not more than –before, and her tail hung limply when she was lifted out of her pen. Pete then held her on her back on a towel, and Jan pushed her hind feet with her fingers, rubbing the muscles around her thighs and gently squeezing her toes.

'We're doing this several times every day at the moment,'

Jan told me. 'I can feel that she does have muscle movement in her legs, she pushes back against me when I do
this, but it's almost as though she's given up trying.'

One thing was for sure: if Kirikoo had given up trying,
then Jan and Pete most certainly had not. They committed
hours of every day working to get her to realise that, with
a bit of effort, she had the capacity to regain the use of
her hindquarters. Watching the couple bent over this little
otter and struggling to get her to respond, I was over-
whelmed by their selfless dedication. For them there was
no question: as long as there was a glimmer of hope, then
everything they could do to help Kirikoo would be done.
But at the same time, I could detect a sadness in them. A
pragmatic realisation that nothing might work and that
they would have to face a terribly difficult decision for
Kirikoo's future. They were up against the clock, too. As
the little otter matured she would grow increasingly intol-
erant of human handling. In a few weeks she would be
aggressive and struggle when held, and that could make
the physiotherapy impossible to administer.

There was nothing wrong with the otter cub's appetite,
and the promise of a bit of fresh fish did encourage a bit
of movement in her back legs as she strained to get the
meal that was placed just out of reach. But my honest
observation after my visit was that she had not improved
in the past few weeks, and if anything had become a little
worse. I was selfishly very glad not to be in Jan and Pete's
position, with the prospect of having to make an impossible decision in the near future.

*

The gloomy weather broke, and with it came an upsurge in activity amongst wild creatures all over the islands. With first light, the moors rang with the calls of golden plover and curlew, and on shingle banks and protected fields, the terns were now settling in to their traditional nesting colonies. With so much happening at the same time, I asked friend and colleague Jamie McPherson to join me, so that we might better cover the flush of spring action with two long-lens cameras. Jamie is a very talented and dedicated wildlife cameraman; his style of fieldwork and shooting echoes that of his – and my – inspiration, Hugh Miles. He is also a first-class chap with a dry wit and ready smile, and that is always invaluable in the face of long, hard days in the field. I particularly wanted Jamie to join me on my next visit to the island of Noss, where I had fixed the remote cameras on the cliff, hoping that gannets would nest within view of it.

We set off for the island on a bright morning with a gentle breeze after several days of strong wind. Chris, the warden, kindly offered to take us in his rubber inflatable to a landing point on the north of the island, reducing our walk with the heavy camera kit by about half a mile. As we neared the sloping rocks that would be our natural jetty, it became increasingly clear that, though the sea was calm, the swell that had built up over the past few days was still significant, rising and falling a good metre or more.

'OK Simon, this is the spot,' Chris said, looking for a good place to push the nose of the boat against the rock and give me an opportunity to hop ashore. Timing would be everything here. If I got it right, I could jump on to the rock almost level with the gunwales of the boat. If not, I could find myself leaping straight into a rock face and down into the sea, or, worse still, be sandwiched between the boat and the jagged shore.

'I'll give it a go. Could you pass me the kit once I'm up there, please?'

Chris had to go around several times before he could line the bow up with a small cleft in the rock. As we neared the shore, I waited for the swell to reach its apex, and hopped on. As I tried to stand I realised the rock face was covered in a slick algae that turned it into a treacherous skidpan.

'Blimey! Bit slippy up here. Right then, let's try to get the kit ashore,' I shouted to the rest of the team in the boat.

Chris made several more passes, and each time Jamie handed another item of the heavy camera gear ashore. At one point, as the boat was leaning against the rocks, a particularly violent swell lifted and tipped it alarmingly. Chris, who was standing at the time, trying to pass me a bag, almost fell in, but fortunately managed to right himself and step back into the boat.

'This is getting a bit hairy,' he said with understated concern. 'Let's get you ashore, Jamie.'

Once we were both on terra (not so) firma, we loaded the kit on to our backs and tottered over the slippery rocks. We both knew from bitter experience that a fall with the gear could lead to very unpleasant injuries, and so took baby steps to reach safer ground.

Having gathered our composure, we briskly set off up the hill. Jamie is immensely fit and about half my age, and I struggled to keep up with his pace, but once into the stride, enjoyed the blood-pumping exercise. We were soon nearing the Noup, the name given to the great sweeping cliff where the gannets nest, and the spot where my remote cameras were positioned.

'If you could pick up some shots of the gannets coming in to the colony, please, I'll see how the nest-cams are doing,' I suggested to Jamie as I made my way to the point where the ends of the camera wires had been hidden for the past few months.

All looked to be in order when I lifted the flat slab of rock on the cliff top that hid and protected the cables and plugs from the nibbling attention of the island's rabbits. I pulled the recording deck and monitor from my kit bag and plugged one of the two camera wires into it. This was the moment of truth. Had gannets chosen to nest on the ledge next to the camera? Was any of the equipment still working? I applied the power source to the system and squinted at the monitor.

'Yay! It's working! And there's a pair of gannets right next to it. Brilliant!'

My initial excitement began to wane as I studied the quality of the image. This was the camera that had the side view of the nest, looking along the ledge to the colony behind. Its position was spot-on: the sitting bird filling centre frame, a second nest beyond, and the cliff face covered in hundreds more beyond that again. But – and it was a big 'but' – it looked as though something had sneezed on the lens. The whole image was milky and obscured.

'Blast!', I muttered, or words to that effect.

It seemed as though a combination of condensation and guano – the former internal; the latter external – had rendered the image unusable. I recorded a little of the output, more for posterity, and to do a technical check in more controlled conditions later, than as an aesthetically pleasing view. As the tape was running, the other member of the pair flew in to land on the ledge with some nesting material in its beak. Watching the lovely behaviour play out, in full view, hidden by a shroud of goo, was just too frustrating. Even more frustrating was the fact that it was becoming obvious that a good percentage of the fault was indeed caused by internal condensation. This from a camera whose suppliers claimed it was rainproof. A tiny bit of moisture had somehow broken through the seals, and that was enough to render the output useless. Getting down the cliff to clean the lens housing was not an option now that the birds were on their nests. On the plus side, the longer I left the camera switched on, the clearer the image became. The small amount of heat generated inter-nally by the power to the unit was sufficient to start demisting the view. But though it was an improvement, it was still well below acceptable standards.

'One down, one to go,' I muttered as I exchanged the input for the wire that led to the camera pointing down at the nest from above. The image on the screen flickered into life and I could see immediately that the view from this one was significantly clearer than from the first. It was bang on target for framing, too, with the sitting bird filling the centre-right of frame and the sheer cliff dropping away to the sea about five hundred feet below. This camera also had a degree of condensation build-up, but after ten minutes or so had cleared enough to get a pretty reasonable shot.

From this 'bird's-eye view' of the nest, I watched what I took to be the female of the pair fiddling with something beneath her feet, reaching down with her beak to adjust nest material and, I hoped, an egg. Her partner returned regularly, his beak stuffed with nesting material. This was sometimes in the form of a strand of seaweed that he must have found floating at sea, but more often he brought great tufts of grass. These he had been plucking from the top of a nearby rock stack that had sufficient soil on top to encourage grass growth, known as the Holm of Noss. A steady stream of gannets was flying in to land on the stack and wrench beaks-full of the stuff to add as a premium building material to their nest mounds. In fact, 'building' is a generous description of what constitutes the forming of a gannet nest. The material that is gathered to build the mound is loosely dropped and then pulled into a rough circular heap, which then is compressed and moulded by the sitting bird's feet and breast. After a while, a substantial clutter of mixed materials builds up, in the centre of which a shallow depression is created through the constant paddling and turning of the sitting bird. This is where the single egg is laid and the chick is raised. Virtually anything is used as nest material, including man's cast-offs, and many structures contain plastic bags, multicoloured nylon rope and shreds of fishing net. To my eyes, it is ugly proof of our careless disregard for our planet and our natural neighbours. The gannets find the plastic cast-offs irresistible, sometimes to their mortal cost. The unyielding modern plastics can entangle their legs and feet, and every year birds die in a grisly, drawn-out struggle to escape the very structure that was built to bring new life into the world.

The nest that my remote camera was trained on seemed mercifully free of man-made materials and was certainly substantial enough not to warrant too much more to keep it in good shape. Not that finishing a nest was guarantee that it would stay in one piece. Gannets have a tendency to pilfer material from their neighbours' nest mounds and, if a structure is left unguarded even for a few minutes, its rightful owners are likely to return to a much-diminished home. That is one reason that from this point, through to at least the early summer, at least one of the pair would now guard the egg – and, in a few weeks, the chick – around the clock. Both parents take turns in incubation and care of their offspring. It is vital, then, that the parents' relationship is rock solid, and this bond is affirmed again and again throughout the nesting season with formal and elaborate displays.

Each time the male arrived with a new offering of nest material, his mate stood up on the nest to greet him, lifting her head and shaking it from side to side. He returned the gesture and dropped the material for her to pull in close to her breast. They then bill-fenced, gently tapping the tips of their beaks against each other, heads held in an angle pointing slightly up, exposing the graphic stripes and marking around their faces and necks. The fencing over, the pair then often mutually preened. This phase of the greeting ritual serves a practical purpose, each member of the pair gently nibbling the feathers on the neck and face of its partner, probably reducing their burden of parasites and certainly helping to keep the plumage in good order in a place that is impossible for each of them to reach alone. The display looks to our eyes very affectionate, and it may well have a profound emotional effect on the birds, but it is also a mechanical safeguard against constant and extreme violence. Gannets nest in close-knit colonies, in large part to reduce the effects of predation from gulls and skuas. A nest alone is far more vulnerable than one defended by thousands of stabbing beaks. But gannets are not naturally friendly neighbours. It is as though each of them has opted to nest close to the next to maximise the defence of its egg and chick, but has done so in extreme sufferance of the deal. Neighbouring birds are quarrelsome and aggressive to each other, and one that strays on to another's patch is attacked with extreme force. Fights can be bloody and, on rare occasions, fatal. Here on Noss, the nests are along the cliff ledges, and a nest territory reaches just as far as a bird sitting in the centre of its mound of material can reach by stretching its neck and beak. In another gannet colony where I have filmed in the past, on the Bass Rock off the Scottish east coast, thousands of birds nest on the gentle slopes on top of the island. An aerial view of the colony reveals near perfect symmetry of spacing, every bird surrounded in a circle by just enough space for it to reach to the outstretched beak of its neighbour.

Back in the nest on Noss, the greeting ceremony was over and the male bird looked to be trying to have a turn incubating the egg, fidgeting close to his mate and staring at what lay beneath her breast every time she rose to her feet. She was having none of it, though, and after a while he grew bored of trying and decided to leave for more building material. Getting away from the nest is a tricky exercise in a gannet colony. A leaving bird is very likely to stray, albeit briefly, into a neighbour's territory and get attacked. To show that they are off, and have no intention of stealing any nest material or indeed attempting to flirt with their neighbour, they adopt a ritualised posture called sky-pointing. My male now walked to the edge of the ledge, his head and neck stretched high, beak pointing straight up at the sky. A second's pause, and he was off, dropping out of view. The sky-point is a very visual signal of intent, but it may also have its roots in a very practical and honest message. Gannets fight with their dagger-shaped beaks. By lifting their weapon to the sky they make a clear statement: 'Don't attack me, I'm unarmed.' It's the equivalent of us walking out of a hostile situation with our hands up and our pockets turned out.

Despite the disappointment of one camera in the nest being virtually unusable and the second being a bit below par, I was still thrilled to be able to spy on their family life in this way. It was possible to look across at some of the nests from a distance, as Jamie was doing further along the cliff top using a long lens, but there is something

The close family bond between a mother otter and her cubs can last more than a year.

Fish are usually their favourite food, but otters can make short work of crabs too.

Alison Pinkney filming us watching puffins at Hermaness. Almost as far north as you can get in the British Isles.

A xylophone in a boat? What's so strange about that?

A bus shelter, Unst style. Very pink.

What's so funny?

Savannah full of energy in Lerwick.

Savannah out for the count on Noss.

Brydon Thomason and me on the Julie Rose, heading past Muckle Flugga, looking for killer whales.

Not killer whales, but white-sided dolphins. Hundreds of them!

Preparing to dive with my 'flatulent' gloves.

The Giant's Leg on Bressay. Impressive above water,
awesome beneath the waves.

'Hello . . .Yes, it's definitely broken . . . It'll take how long to fix?'
Me with broken viewfinder for the slow motion camera.

Our saviours!

Gannet fest, Noss.

special about getting a camera close to the action. It makes everything you see more intimate somehow, more personal. I looked forward to coming back in a few weeks to see if the pair had hatched their chick. With enough material recorded from the nest-cam, I packed the gear and walked along the cliff to where Jamie had been filming more general activity with the gannets. He was pleased with what he had seen, having recorded courtship, fights, nest building and birds tending their eggs. We decided to film the grass being gathered by a constantly shifting flock of gannets from the top of the nearby rock stack, and wandered down the slope to get a better vantage point. As we approached the lower slopes we noticed puffins sitting on a low stone wall. Having spent the winter at sea, they too were getting on with preparations for breeding and, in the colonies all around Shetland, their numbers were building rapidly.

We decided to redirect our efforts at trying to record some of the puffins' breeding preparation and set up our filming gear close to the wall. There is a part of me that wants to be a bird-watching maverick, and say that I can't understand what all the fuss is about when it comes to puffins. They are undoubtedly one of Britain's favourite birds, and their colourful, clownish images adorn myriad magazine covers, promotional posters, mugs, T-shirts — you name it. I want to say that, but I can't, because, like everyone else, I find them adorable. I have no doubt that a large part of their appeal stems from our anthropomorphic projections on their character and form. As a puffin waddles pompously over a grassy cliff top, it is impossible not to think of a rather portly old gentleman, whose taste for drink has enlarged and coloured his nose. His white chest is absurdly puffed up to project through his neat, black waistcoat, and he wears ridiculous, bright orange shoes and spats. Then there are the clownish elements – the brightly marked eye and the red-tinted beak – that further add to our association of human qualities with the bird. They even make a sound that is faintly human: a low and nasal utterance, as though they have seen a rather risqué image, like an older gentleman responding to some juicy gossip: ooo, oooooooohhhhh.

The puffins moved away a little as we got the camera gear organised, but after five minutes were settling back around the wall. I realised that there were a number of burrows in the ground close to where we were sitting and that this was the reason the birds were gathered here. Puffins are generally confiding birds and, in the past, and even to this day on some parts of their range, this trust in man has been their downfall. They were once harvested for their meat on Shetland. Now they are fully protected by law in Britain, and thankfully in Shetland their trust of man, so abused in the past, persists and is now justified. There are three main spots where anyone can see them at close quarters: Sumburgh Head in the south, Hermaness in the north and Noss, where we now sat, in the east. The colony here on the cliff top was by no means the biggest in the islands, with less than two thousand pairs compared to twenty thousand on the island of Foula. But it was definitely one of the most convenient and intimate for filming. Jamie and I were careful not to sit too close to a burrow so that we didn't put any birds off visiting and prospecting for nesting places. But we stayed close enough to ensure we could get intimate views of the complex behaviour they were displaying around the nest sites.

All around us, the dumpy little birds began to waddle closer, and within ten minutes we had at least fifteen puffins within ten metres. On the rock stack opposite, where the gannets had been collecting grass, a club of non-breeding birds had gathered and were going through the motions of courtship and display. Puffins usually pair for life, so the decision of which mate to pick has major implications on their breeding success and future. A lot of time is invested in picking the right male, or female, in puffin society, and birds may not breed for three years or more after they leave the nest, returning to the colonies in the spring to get together with other singles and make a choice. Today, clubs of five or six birds formed loose rings, occasionally flicking their heads and using their colourful beaks as flags. Now and again, a male approached a female and the two would bill-fence, clattering their broad beaks one against the other and then breaking off abruptly, looking for all the world as though they had been caught in the middle of a passionate kiss and were a little embarrassed. Elsewhere, older, established pairs had fast-tracked their courtship and were in the process of preparing a nest burrow, one of the great advantages of having already decided with whom they were going to mate and raise a chick. For many, the burrow would be a hole in the ground they had prepared and used in previous seasons, or else old rabbit burrows in need of renovation.

There seemed to be a housing shortage this year, and we filmed several squabbles over which bird had the right to use prime real estate. Here and there, new burrows were being dug, and we saw a graphic illustration of one of the practical purposes of their comically deep and powerful beaks. Birds (when we were filming these were always males) lay on their chest and worked at a shallow depression in the soil, with their beaks digging and twisting the soil away as we might if using a pick-axe. When sufficient loose soil had been peeled away from the back of the burrow, the powerful webbed feet and claws were deployed to shovel the earth behind the digging bird. This industry sometimes attracted the close attention of what we took to be the female of the pair, who would lean in to inspect the work. More than once, she received a face full of soil as she did so. It was impossible not to think of this as a deliberate 'accidentally on purpose' display of indignation on the part of her mate.

Using another mini cam (this time with no condensation or guano as a filter), I crept close to a pair of birds that were sitting by the entrance to their burrow. I managed to get the camera within twenty centimetres of the nearest bird, and record some fun low-angle views against the blue sky.

Eggs would soon be laid in the underground retreats, one per pair, and the chicks within be raised through the spring and summer. I wanted to try and reveal this hidden part of their world, and to that end had done a great deal of preparatory work during our winter trip in February at some of the nest burrows in the Sumburgh colony. Together with RSPB wardens Helen Moncrieff and Pete Ellis, we had inspected a number of burrows that might be suitable for introducing a mini camera and infrared lights. We had decided on a few and introduced lengths of plastic piping that could house the filming equipment later in the year and so reduce the level of disturbance we would impose once the nests were occupied. Even though puffins can be very confiding above ground, they can also be very jumpy when they are on the nest. Undue attention to birds sitting on an egg can cause them to abandon: a completely unacceptable result and counter-productive to the goal of revealing their nesting behaviour. With a number of nests ready to take a camera later in the year, we would wait until the chicks had hatched and were reasonably well grown before taking a peek, and, we hoped, recording an otherwise little understood and rarely seen facet of their lives.

It would be several weeks before that ambition could become a reality, and in the meantime there was a great deal more happening on the islands that I wanted to record.

# Chapter 13

## Family Fortunes

It had been a while since I had visited the otter family on the lagoon, and I wanted to see how the family of the mum with three cubs was getting on. On my last visit, it had been clear that there were still strong ties between the youngsters and their mum, but that all of the otters were well equipped to fend for themselves so their desire to be close to their mother was an emotional rather than a practical one.

We still had about half a mile of walking over the heather moorland to go before we reached the lagoon when we heard the first piping calls of an otter cub. I was with John, who had kindly volunteered to help spot with me, and Marguerite who was filming us, and we all crouched low, trying to get a fix on the source of the sound. Scanning the opposite hillside, I picked out the ginger-brown form of an otter curled up on a grassy bank. Through the camera I could see it was in fact two otters, the mother and her male cub, which now looked bigger than her. He was nestling close to his mum and trying to suckle, and she was not amused. When he pushed her too far, she whipped around and bit him on the head and nose and this set him off on the series of self-pitying, high-pitched squeaks that had caught our attention.

'He's a bit big to be trying that, isn't he, John?' I whispered.

John studied the pair through his binoculars. 'No wonder she's fed up with him. Not long now before she'll have had enough, I reckon.'

The cub continued to try and get close to his mum and she would allow his contact up to a point, but the moment he tried to suckle she turned on him aggressively, whickering and baring her teeth.

Eventually, her patience snapped and, disentangling herself from his embrace, she ran to a tiny freshwater burn where she disappeared, heading for the lagoon. For a moment or two, the cub sniffed the ground where she had been, then, calling continuously, ran after her.

We too got to our feet, following at a distance, and by the time the adult female had reached the water, her cub had caught up with her. The mother looked none too pleased about the arrival of her whining shadow, but there didn't seem to be much she could do about him.

We watched them catching small fish in the lagoon for a while, and then they headed up over the shingle bar. Arctic terns were now nesting on the top of the long pebble beach that separated the lagoon from the voe, and the whole colony rose up in swearing alarm as the otter pair trotted up and over their refuge. Otters can, and do from time to time, take young ground-nesting birds and eggs, and I wondered what if any future the terns here had with such intensive otter traffic.

We lost contact with the pair for a while after that, and decided to take to the high ground to scan for them or any other otters in the area, John heading up around the coast to the north, leaving Marguerite and me overlooking the lagoon. We still had not seen the two female cubs, or the mature dog that patrolled this stretch of coast. After an hour or so, I spotted an otter swimming out on to the far side of the lagoon. I used the walkie-talkie to let John know what we'd seen and, with Marguerite, moved down the hill to try and get a closer view and identify which otter this was.

We reached the cover of the peat bank on the eastern shore of the lagoon just in time to hear a cub whistling nearby. I scanned the far bank with binoculars and picked up an otter running down from the little burn. It was followed by another, slightly larger, that was constantly calling. This was our female and the male cub. They had somehow doubled back unseen, and it looked as if the mother was still doing her very best to shake off her nagging youngster. They entered the water and swam to the far side of the lagoon, in the direction of a large peat bank where I knew they had a holt. The female emerged first, running up the grassy slope, closely followed by her cub. Just as he was about to come parallel with his mum, she turned on him, holding her head low and opening her mouth in an aggressive gape. Her shrill, wavering call left nothing to doubt; a reasonable translation might be: 'If you don't stop following me, I'm going to give you such a hiding you'll be sore for weeks!'

This was the very break of the family fabric I had wanted to witness, and now that it was so graphically before me, I felt for the cub. For the past year or so he had been nurtured, fed and cared for by his mother. She had been the centre of his world and virtually everything he had learned had been in her company. I could imagine his confusion now that this nurturing figure was turning on him in such a hostile way. It was all for his own good, of course: tough love, otter style. If he stuck around much longer there would be new conflicting feelings stirring in him that he might direct towards his mother, and that was not something she would tolerate. As a male, he would also represent a threat to the dominant dog in the territory and, even though this would almost certainly be his father, he would be given short shrift if he were caught trying to stay in the neighbourhood once he was sexually mature.

Suitably cowed, the male cub watched his mum run up the bank and then slowly crept along the shoreline below her. More otter calls to the south caught my attention and I turned the camera to reveal a third, then a fourth otter swimming up to the opposite bank. It was the two female cubs, determined to find out what all the noise was about.

Emboldened by the arrival of his sisters, the young male climbed to where his mother was just slipping out of sight into a hole on the top of the peat bank. He was joined by his sisters, and all three sniffed around the entrance, calling wistfully for their mum.

As I filmed the event, I realised I was witnessing a pivotal moment in these animals' lives, and just how lucky I was to be here on this day. So much of my professional life is spent waiting for the unexpected, the elusive, the shy and the rare.

Simply catching a glimpse of a wild otter is, for most

people, an enormous thrill. I too can watch one in deep slumber, or bobbing on the water's surface chewing a butterfish, and still feel a similar sense of awe as I did the first time I ever set eyes on one, more than thirty years ago: a shadow cutting a line across a sunset lake on the Somerset Levels. But how much more satisfaction I gained now, not just in 'seeing' my subjects, but learning to understand them. The more intimate the knowledge, the greater the prize. Spending time watching an animal is one thing. Knowing it as an individual, seeing it interact with others, playing, fighting, foraging and, on this occasion, splitting apart from its family, is the ultimate goal. This was the prize that justified the many hours of cold, wet, uncomfortable and sometimes exhausting effort that went into watching and recording the wild spirits with which we share this world.

All three cubs fussed around the entrance to the holt, none brave enough to try and enter. Once or twice I saw why they might be nervous, as their mother lunged at their noses if they got too close, her head briefly popping out of the hole, then disappearing just as quickly. After about twenty minutes, the cubs started to calm down and began a gentle grooming session, close to the holt entrance. The mother saw this as her chance and started to emerge from the holt, head low, body language full of tension and hostility. I thought I was going to witness her last savage rebuff of her offspring, but, as is so often the case with the social life of wild creatures, she surprised me. I think she surprised her cubs too. After slowly walking behind each of them she relented and stopped to groom first her son, then one of her daughters. The contact was short and cursory by otter standards, but it was a benign gesture on her part, perhaps the first for days or even weeks. It's impossible to know what was going through her head, of course. Perhaps she too was having a difficult time, experiencing a period of conflicting emotions. I use the latter word with intent, and am prepared to defend it.

Anthropomorphism, the reading of human emotion into another creature's psyche and behaviour, is unwise. But to think that we are the only animals on earth to have emotions is equally fatuous. Emotions drive us to do the things we do to survive. If we go without food for a few days we are hungry, of course, but we are also stressed and anxious and these emotions drive us to source a meal ever more eagerly.

The feelings of love we have for a partner are part of an essential mechanism in the process of procreation. We feel love, of a very different kind, for our children too. Paternal or maternal love is perhaps the most powerful of all the base emotions, and I find it curious that, as far as I'm aware, no language has developed a different word to describe it. It is so powerful that we might readily put our own lives on the line to protect those of our offspring. It is the height of human arrogance to assume we are alone on this earth when it comes to emotions. They are the tools of evolution, and I have no doubt that most, if not all of our fellow mammals, and quite probably other creatures too, are guided, compelled and confused by emotions on a daily basis.

As I watched the mother otter 'giving in' and finally

relenting by grooming her family, I wondered what feelings she was having to manage. The process of separation
from these three young animals to which she had devoted
her energy, indeed her entire life, for the past year or so,
must have been a stressful one for her too. Her biological,
instinctive drive to shun them, now that she was preparing
to start a new family, must at times have been – at the
very least – confusing and even unpleasant for her.

For a minute or two the whole family rolled on the
grass bank, the male cub especially revelling in his mother's
attention, but she soon tired of the contact, lifted her
head and trotted down over the bank to the sea, with all
three of her big cubs in tow.

It was to be the last time I would ever see them together.

Following the otter family was a singular pursuit, but it
did not blinker me to the extent that I was unaware of
the marvels of the other wildlife around the lagoon. As
we waited for an otter to show up, sitting in the heather
scanning the water below, a mountain hare would often
watch us, or an arctic tern would pause in its flight to the
colony to swoop at our heads and swear a brief warning.
The lagoon itself was used by rafts of eider duck, the
dandy black and white drakes vying for the attention of
the drab brown females. Whenever I hear eiders calling,
I can't help but smile. If a puffin call resembles a surprised
gentleman, then the eider is his equally surprised, gossiping
wife. Think of the cliché of two ladies leaning over a
garden fence and reacting to a choice titbit of local scandal
and you have the eider call to a 'T'. OooooOOoooh! It

starts low, rises in the middle and falls again at the end, and is so human in tone that I have had colleagues in the field asking me what I just said, when in fact I have been silent and it has been the ducks doing all the talking.

The drakes' display is punctuated by this call, but is also strikingly visual and ritualised, with sudden throws of the head up over the back, showing off the pied markings and splash of pastel green on the head and neck to greatest effect.

Common seals paused from time to time to stare at us as we crouched in the rocks, their powers of observation significantly more acute than those of their otter neighbours. But it was the red-throated divers that had charisma and allure enough to draw my attention away from the search for otters completely from time to time. At least two pairs regularly visited the sea loch to fish, flying down from their nesting sites on the hill, announcing their arrival with guttural, staccato, goose-like calls. Their Shetland name is rain goose, referring to the belief that when you hear one calling, it's going to rain. In Shetland you're on to a fairly safe bet with this one!

Once on the loch they would colour the sound-scape with their haunting cries and, from time to time, the two pairs would come together to argue about which had the fishing rights to the bay. These disputes were rare, but full of style and beauty when they did kick off, and would end with each of the pairs reaffirming their bonds with a ritualised display that involved paddling hard over the water with their feet, bodies raised and wings closed to their sides, head and neck arched to point down at the surface; all the time uttering the sounds of wilderness.

# Chapter 14

## Into the Deep

There was a whole facet of Shetland wildlife which hitherto had remained hidden from me: that which thrived
beneath the waves. I knew the isles had a reputation for
teeming marine life, and equally well knew that the only
way to explore it was to get beneath the surface. For
millions of people, diving is a leisure sport, and I can
understand why. But my own diving experience, which is
modest but spread over twenty years of learning, has almost
exclusively been in my line of work as a wildlife film-
maker. In fact, some of the first forays I ever made under
water were filming an otter in a flooded quarry in Scotland
for one of the *Animal Dramas* I made annually with my
late father. My instructor and dive supervisor back then
was an ebullient chap by the name of Richard Bull. His
enormous breadth and depth of experience had been added
to over the years on countless projects, many of which
were the backbone of epic productions like *The Blue Planet*
and *Planet Earth*. With little hope of finding him available, the production team asked if he would be prepared
to supervise the diving I wanted to do in Shetland, and I
was delighted by his positive response.

A plan was hatched for Richard, together with top underwater cameraman Gavin Newman, to join me in the north,

and together we would make a series of dives around the isles, hopefully illustrating some of the marine riches. I wanted to get in the water before the summer had an opportunity to colour the seas with any bloom of plankton, but not so early that life had not yet properly blossomed. The middle of May seemed an ideal time, and so all plans aimed at us having the equipment, dive team, boat and the research on dive sites prepared by then.

When the time came, we had the dive team, boat and dive site research in place. Richard and Gavin had arrived and were installed in their hotel in Lerwick, and local boatman Bernie was on standby to take us out the moment the sea conditions allowed. As it turned out, it was not the weather that scuppered our well-laid plans, but a confusion with a courier service that was supposed to have shipped my diving kit to Shetland days earlier, but so far still had not. This was a problem. Diving, like so many things, is an activity as strong as the weakest link in its chain. As well as a personally fitted dry suit, my gear included a special dive mask that enabled me to talk whilst under water, and a number of other personal items with which I was familiar. With everyone waiting for me, we had to do some rapid creative thinking to come up with a Plan B, and quickly. This is where Richard comes into his own. He will never compromise on safety, but his no-nonsense, can-do attitude has saved numerous underwater film shoots from going down the plughole, if you'll excuse the pun. He spoke with Bernie the boatman, and overnight pulled together enough gear to ensure we could get in the water the following day. I would not be able to talk once

I was down there, but some would argue maybe that was a blessing.

We decided our first dive would be from shore, simply to test the kit and iron out any minor gremlins that might arise, without the added hassle of having to get in and out of a boat. We chose a site on the east coast and all met at the car park of an old church close to the shore. Whilst Gavin dressed in his personalised gear, I joined Bernie at the side of his Transit van to inspect what kit I might be using. Various fellow divers had very generously leant their gear for the day, and I was handed workman-like dry suits, BC (buoyancy compensator), air, pony cylinder and all the other bits and bobs needed to get under the surface safely. I had with me one piece of gear I knew would not have been considered necessary. A nappy. Before your imagination runs into any vulgar corner, let me explain. Certainly many dry suits do not make the task of relieving yourself very easy. Their waterproof zips are set across the back of your shoulders (as was the zip in the one I was borrowing), making it tricky if not down-right impossible to undo it without someone's help. But getting caught short was not my reason for wanting a nappy to hand. Dry suits do what it says on the box: they keep you dry. A warm layer of clothing beneath the water-proof outer layer stays cosy enough to work in freezing waters for protracted dives. Most people using a dry suit tend to stay in the prone, or swimming position, and though you expel a great deal of the air from the suit as you dive, there is inevitably a little left within, which helps with insulation and buoyancy. In the prone position this air tends to rise to a strip along your back and the overall fit is very comfortable. BUT. If, like me and many other people who film under water, you spend most of your time in the upright position, perhaps kneeling on the sea bed, or else standing hidden in a kelp garden with both hands on the camera and eye to the eyepiece, the air in your dry suit tends to gather in the highest point, i.e. your shoulders. Not a problem for your torso, arms or shoulders, but the lower part of the suit becomes compressed with water pressure and very tight around your feet, ankles, legs and, yes, you guessed it. Female underwater camera operators don't suffer any undue effects of this 'squeeze', but I had learnt from very uncomfortable and bitter experience that unless a suit was made to fit me perfectly, there was a good chance I would spend an hour or so with my groin being held in a vice-like grip, and I would emerge with my voice having risen an octave. And that's where the nappy came in. Carefully placed, it would provide a cushion against the crushing effects of water pressure, and give me one less thing to think about.

I stepped into my borrowed dry suit and pulled the rubber neck seal over my head. As Bernie zipped me in, I immediately knew that the amount of time I could spend in this suit would be limited. One of the reasons a suit tends to be customised for the individual is that the important seals around the wrists and neck must fit perfectly. Too loose and they let water in. Too tight and they restrict blood flow. This suit was doing the latter. It would have been too much to ask that someone cut their personalised seal to suit me, so I made no noise and got on with pulling the rest of my kit on, from weight belt to buoyancy compensator jacket with air tank and ancillary kit. I'm not fond of this bit of the dive preparation. My dislike has nothing to do with any sense of anxiety; it's the increasingly encumbered state you find yourself in prior to jumping in the water. My clumsy, weighed-down stagger to the water's edge could not have been more different from the lithe athleticism of an otter trotting over land. By the time I reached the beach, it felt as if my head was going to explode, so tight was the neck seal, but I knew that once I was in the water the pressure would ease and I would be able to breathe more freely. I hoped so, anyway.

Our shore dive was uneventful from the wildlife point of view, with nothing more than a few starfish and small crabs on which to test the cameras that Gavin and I were using. We finned around for about an hour and then headed back to shore. When we reached the land, Marguerite came to greet me.

'Did you see it? It was right next to you!' she asked excitedly.

'See what?' I responded suspiciously, half suspecting a wind-up.

'The otter! Oh, what a shame, it looked from here like it was swimming down to check out your bubbles; it was very relaxed.'

I was still a bit unsure whether to believe this tale, but a careful look into her eyes betrayed the truth: we had been investigated by a wild otter and neither Gavin nor I had been aware of it.

Much as I enjoy many elements of diving, this lack of

agility and freedom to look around is another of my frustrations with it. Above surface, I can use all my senses to detect a wild creature, from the sounds it makes to the flicker of movement it might cause in my peripheral vision. Even though modern dive gear has vastly improved on much of the stuff I learned in, it is still compromising when it comes to peripheral vision and spotting creatures in the 360-degree environment of the deep. Often a subject has to swim straight in front of you to be seen. This, and the heavy gear associated with SCUBA (self-contained underwater breathing apparatus) diving are reasons why, when I enter the undersea world for pleasure, I prefer to free dive. I don't do this in a competitive fashion, and I have very limited experience. I am also no master of the breath-hold, but even getting to the sea bed twenty metres down and sitting with the fish for forty seconds or so wearing nothing more than a pair of trunks, a mask, a snorkel and a few weights on a belt is so much more liberating and in touch with the underwater element than wrapping up in all the SCUBA kit. The trouble is, I have to come back to the surface to breathe every couple of minutes or so, and that is once I have been training for a while. Compare that to the world human breath-hold record of over eleven minutes, and you'll realise why I feel inadequate in the discipline. Even so, the forty seconds or so when I can sit on a sandy sea bed, with no sound of air bubbles rattling in my ears and the freedom to wriggle around as best my human form allows, is as close as I think I will ever get to the feeling enjoyed by an otter.

'What's wrong with your face?' Marguerite looked

concerned as I removed my hood and mask. 'You look like you're about to explode!'

I was very relieved to be out of the dry suit and have normal service resume to the blood flow in my head. Most of the gear had worked perfectly, and a search for a new dry suit turned up the perfect fit whilst my own kit was still in transit.

We decided the next dive should be a little more adventurous, and the next day, with overcast but calm conditions, we headed out of Lerwick harbour and north along the coastline. En route, we passed Shetland Catch, a huge fish-processing plant on the outskirts of town. On the exposed rocks below the giant warehouse, a gang of twenty or so grey seals were hauled out, enjoying a break from their aquatic lifestyle. All were bulls, and quite probably benefited from occasional fish scraps that found their way into the sea here. Certainly, some of the returning fishing boats would throw scraps into the water as they approached port, and the seals knew where best to intercept a likely meal. We slowed the boat as we approached and Bernie's deckhand for the day prepared a couple of pollack heads he had brought in a crate for this very eventuality.

'Come on then,' he shouted to the now curious seals and lobbed his offering into the water. The whole mob shuffled their great bulks down the rocks and into the water. Before long we were surrounded by their dog-like faces, staring up at us from the surface and hoping for another titbit to be thrown. They were not disappointed and one even came to the stern of the boat to take a fish from Jim's hand. 'Let's hop in and see if we can film them under water,' I suggested.

Gavin joked that he was going to stuff a few fish down the back of my neck to make me extra-specially attractive as we dressed in the gear, and within minutes we were both in the water and finning slowly towards the nearest seal.

It was immediately obvious that these animals were not used to divers. There are communities of grey seals elsewhere in Britain that are so confiding they will nip your fins and swim up to your mask for some eye-to-eye contact. They have every reason to feel confident; as the largest mammal in Britain to come on land, a bull can weigh three hundred kilos and is equipped with a mouthful of sharp, powerful teeth, more than a match for any human. But this group of seals was cautious. Perhaps it was just the novelty of our actions; perhaps they had suffered some persecution in the past – certainly, despite legal protection, grey and common seals are still the victims of unlicensed and illegal killings from time to time.

We spent a good twenty minutes in the shallow water near the seals, but in all that time only filmed fleeting glimpses of their giant forms through the murk of the silt they stirred with their movements. After a while, Gavin and I surfaced and decided to steam to new pastures rather than use up precious dive time on a lost cause.

Once we were back on board, we set sail for a point further north that had a reputation for being rich with underwater invertebrate life. After a journey of about half an hour we anchored up within fifty metres of the shore, where the land dropped sharply into the sea. Armed with camera and lights, Gavin and I jumped in and followed the anchor line to the sea bed, then made our way across to the shoreline at a depth of about fifteen metres. Along the way we noticed increasing numbers of starfish and crabs lurking amongst the weed and rocks and, since it was still early enough in the season for the algae to be fairly stunted in growth, we were afforded a clear view of the sea bed and anything that lived there. General water clarity was pretty good, too, and we could see for about ten metres or so. At a point where the rocks started to rise up to form a wall we slowed our pace and began to investigate the myriad nooks and crevices more closely. Gavin signalled towards something he had found on a large boulder, and I drifted to join him, looking down to see a large sun star, about twenty centimetres across and a vivid orange in colour. Nearby, a velvet swimming crab retreated to its lair as we swam overhead, and a delicate decorator crab, so called because they take little bits of algae and stick them to their body for camouflage, walked over a strand of weed with long-legged grace. Mindful of having missed the otter on the earlier dive, I finned back away from the rock face and turned to scan the water and surface behind us. The check was timely, for I was presented with a truly awesome spectacle.

The current and tide had washed a vast wave of life into the bay; a swarm of moon jellyfish stretched as far as I could see, gently pulsating, translucent bodies creating a living curtain between us and the surface. For the most part, diving with air is a means to an end for me, a way of exploring an alien environment that would otherwise be out of reach. The many extraordinary things I have witnessed in the watery world have justified the clumsy, inelegant process it has taken to enter it. But just occasionally I have found myself completely forgetting about the paraphernalia required to access the marine environment and have become one with the three-dimensional element. This was one of those moments. I rose up from the sea bed until I was completely surrounded by the jellies. There, in mid-water, I was able to move slowly in any direction, travelling weight-lessly through a galaxy of living forms, drifting with them with the forces of the current. Moon jellyfish are simple creatures, with a weak sting that rarely penetrates a human skin. Their pulsating swimming action serves only to keep them near the surface or change their position in the water column; it is too weak to propel them against the current and tide and so they are at the whim of the weather, flow and tide of the sea. They are common in British waters in the summer months, but this was a spectacularly large swarm, especially for so early in the season.

Once back at the surface, Gavin and I registered our mutual pleasure at having serendipitously found the jellies and swam back to the boat, where a welcome hot cup of tea and sandwiches had been prepared.

'Excellent, really excellent. Best jelly swarm I've seen for ages,' Gavin enthused as he pulled the heavy tank and belt from his body.

Given that he spent most of his professional life under water, I took this as proof positive that we had seen something very special indeed.

*

We had to wait a day to make the final dive on my wish list, and on the morning of that final opportunity to get in the water, my diving gear turned up. Better late than never! By now, we had refined the loaned gear to fit me, and it would have taken longer to test and trim the custom-made dry suit than to stick with what I had been using for the past few days. But now, at last, we had the full face mask with microphone that would allow me to communicate with the surface and create a verbal record of whatever I saw. Fittingly, we had saved what promised to be the best dive until last.

At the southern end of Bressay island, opposite Lerwick, was a famed dive site known as the Giant's Leg. This great sandstone arch was big enough to navigate a large boat through at the surface, and the 'leg' extended fifteen metres or more below. Such a striking geological feature would be fun to swim through on an aesthetic level, but we had information suggesting the vertical rock faces harboured some weird and wonderful life forms too. The water here, as elsewhere in Shetland, was still pretty nippy – about ten degrees, or less. The use of the dry suits was essential for prolonged dives, and a good pair of gloves kept hands from chilling to the point of immobility. I had been borrowing a pair of customised rubber work gloves from Bernie that were as good, or better, than any purpose-made dive gloves I had used before. They were more usually used by fish-farm workers in winter, with a robust, sealed rubber outer and a fleece inner. To waterproof them, Bernie had added a rubber wrist seal. Simple but very effective. They were a bit of a pickle to get on, and the unavoidable trapped air would make it look as though I had elephantiasis of the hand until I purged them. The latter exercise was done with a twist of the wrist and gentle pressure on the glove, which produced a satisfyingly vulgar sound as the air passed by the rubber seal. I had two built-in whoopee cushions. I guess it was a boy thing, but every time I vented air from the gloves before a dive, it gave me a giggling fit. Little things . . .

Once the boat was anchored and we were dressed in our gear, the communication mask tested and all cameras on standby, we were ready for the dive. Our presence had attracted a spectator in the form of a very confiding bonxie. He was clearly used to people offering him titbits, and watched our movements hopefully, pecking at our air-supply hoses as Gavin and I made our final safety checks at the surface. Then we submerged and set off in the direction of the arch, the bonxie watching us from the surface as we made a slow descent. The water visibility was a little degraded here, tiny particles of silt stirred up by what was a fairly strong current running through the ravine that lay beneath the arch. It was dark, too, sunlight blinkered by the rock structure above us, but I began to see some of the natural jewels others had spoken of, clinging to the sheer rock walls.

Dahlia anemones, thousands of them, appeared like ghostly dead flowers on the vertical faces, the lack of light and depth of water preventing the richness of their colouration from being displayed to its full potential. We switched on our filming lights and were presented with a delicately lovely show of colour. Each of the anemones, simple animals despite their botanical name, bore over a hundred waving tentacles, and these were barred with stripes of violet and orange. I often wonder why such creatures are so richly pigmented, given that they do not migrate close to the surface where red light can permeate and so reveal their splendour. Perhaps the eyes of other creatures can detect details that we cannot; but, in the case of the anemones, they have no eyes, so any finery is strictly for the benefit of, or a warning to, species other than themselves. The dahlias shared their rocky home with another curious beast, a colonial soft coral known as dead man's fingers. These communities of tiny polyps, each armed with eight tentacles, seem to sprout from their anchor on the rocks like small white cacti. Many of the collective masses branch and split into several arms, looking a little like a hand, and the feathery effect of the minute tentacles over their surface gives the impression that they are mouldy and decomposing, hence the aptly descriptive name.

Small fish, crabs, starfish and sun stars added to the animal garden of pigment and form. The ravine offered a relatively weed-free environment, with a constantly shifting current that washed nutrients and small animals within reach of this battery of passive hunters.

It was a wonderful taste of the world explored by the otters, seabirds, seals and cetaceans that I so admired at the surface. When I watched these creatures again in the future, I would have a better idea of this hidden part of their world, and in my imagination would be able to dive with them and explore the dark and life-filled corners of their submarine playground.

Back on the boat, satisfied with our journey beneath the Giant's Leg, we started an obligatory surface break and the journey back to Lerwick. Before calling an end to the diving, I had one last ambition. I had been frustrated by the poor views we had achieved of the grey seals near the port, and hoped that we might be able to improve on them, noting on the journey over the Bressay that a number of common and grey seals were hauled out on the rocks on the western coastline. We made our way back to the spot for a final attempt to film them under water.

The seals were tolerant of the boat anchored about eighty metres from their resting place, and I could only hope they would be equally obliging under water. It was shallow here, no more than ten metres deep, and the sea bed was covered with a dense kelp forest. This was ideal hunting habitat for the seals and provided us with a great place to hide and wait for them to come to within view of the cameras.

Warmed up after a bite to eat and a nice cuppa, Gavin and I were back in the water and swimming towards the shore where the seals had been watching our approach with interest. As well as being able to speak into the full face mask, I could also hear Richard speaking into a microphone at the surface. We made no attempt to bribe these seals, instead hoping their natural curiosity would eventually bring them close enough to film.

About twenty metres from their haul-out, we settled into the kelp bed and waited for a sign. The seals would have been able to see our bubbles coming their way and soon I heard Richard reporting on the status topside.

'Simon, there are quite a few in the water now. They look pretty curious. Every time one surfaces it seems to be a little closer to you, over.'

'Thanks Richard, just seeing shadows at the mo. I'll let you know if they come close enough to see properly.'

We were limited to about fifty minutes of dive time, restricted by the amount of air we had and the safe period we could afford before nitrogen build-up in our blood would threaten us with the bends. Some divers assume that if you stay in shallow water then your 'bottom time' is virtually limitless. But the moment you get in the water and the gases you inhale are even remotely under pressure, you begin to absorb nitrogen into your bloodstream at a rate higher than if you were breathing air at the surface. Indeed, protracted, repeat periods in shallow water can be deceptively dangerous, since the nitrogen has time to 'soak' into the tissues gradually and releases equally gradually. But with Gavin as my dive buddy and Richard at the surface, I knew that all these variables had been properly considered and we were well within our safe zone.

Time and again, I caught a glimpse of a seal drifting through the water just beyond clear visibility. I could see by the shape of their heads that they were common seals, but had noticed one or two female greys on the rocks when we entered the water and hoped that they too would join us. Fifteen minutes into the dive, I began to wonder if we should try and get a little closer to the haul-out, but decided to give it ten more minutes in our kelp forest hide-out before closing the distance. Patience paid off, as a female grey grew suddenly bolder, swimming around us at speed no more than five metres away. She returned to look at me, and perhaps at her own reflection in the camera port, twisting and pirouetting through shafts of yellow sunlight that provided a dramatic stage for her marine ballet. I had filmed seals swimming before, but that didn't detract from the sense of awe at the transformation of these creatures from lumbering land mammals to magnificent marine hunters. The image most of us have of a seal is a big, clumsy creature, barely able to support its own weight, flopping down the beach to the sea when disturbed. But this is the very margin of the seal's world and existence. In the water they are the embodiment of agility and grace. The slightest flick of their hind limbs and digits, which they fan out to expose broad webs that transform into a vertical tail fin like that of a fish, sends them steaming through the water like a torpedo. A simple spread of their forelimbs brings them to an abrupt halt, and their bodies, which above water look stiff and ungainly, become supple and athletic. Above the water, we look at seals with a certain air of physical superiority, but beneath the waves the roles are most certainly reversed. Here, we are the lumbering clumsy fools, and they swim rings around us. Filming the seals dancing before me was a fittingly humbling conclusion to our underwater adventures around the isles.

# Chapter 15

## The World According to Unst

Exploring the underwater world was an ambition realised, but it had meant spending long days away from Savannah. Searching for and filming otters, too, was not yet something our daughter was old enough to share. The huge number of hours spent in the field, difficult physical conditions and long walks, not to mention the need to keep silent for long periods would have been too much to ask of a two and a half year old. I had been able to show her otters from the car when we had spotted one from the road, but following them on foot would have to wait a year or two.

Puffin-watching was another thing altogether. The confiding nature of the birds, together with relatively easy access to some of their breeding colonies, meant that Marguerite and I could plan a trip to take Savannah to see them. Of the handful of accessible nesting colonies on Shetland, the one in the south, at Sumburgh Head, is perhaps the easiest to reach. But it is at the opposite end of the islands, at Hermaness on Unst in the far north, that you find arguably the most dramatic.

We decided to take Savannah with us on a bit of an adventure. Following the otters over the past few days had meant I'd seen very little of her, especially now the lengthening sunlight hours kept me in the field beyond her bedtime and took me out before she woke in the morning. I missed her, and needed to give her some time, for both of us.

On the next fine morning we struck out north, the forecast promising sunshine with the small risk of an occasional light shower. Our rented house was more than halfway up the mainland, but even then the journey to Hermaness would take time. We had to catch two ferries to reach it, the first to Yell, the island where the late Bobby Tulloch once lived, and where Hugh Miles had made his inspirational film about otters many years previously. We then had to drive due north, straight over Yell to the ferry port of Gutcher, home to the Wind Dog Cafe. After travelling for more than an hour and a half, the warmth and hospitality of this simple restaurant – near what feels like the end of the world – is very welcome indeed. We decided to take a short break and lunch, a bowl of soup and a sandwich, whilst waiting for the next ferry to Unst to arrive at the terminal. As I entered the cafe, I spotted Andy Foote, one of the research scientists who had been working on the killer whale project. With Savannah tucking in to her soup, and playing with the books and cuddly toys thoughtfully provided by the owners of the cafe, Andy brought Marguerite and me up to date with some of their findings. Fascinating details of the orcas' social structure were emerging through painstaking study. So fascinating, in fact, that I completely lost track of the time.

'The ferry, it's here!' urged Marguerite.

In a fluster, I tried to get all our things together and

into the car, but by the time we were in a position to drive on to the boat, it was too late, it was pulling away from the terminal without us. At least we had the opportunity for a more leisurely lunch now.

After forty-five minutes, we were in the car and properly prepared to catch the next ferry to Unst, the most northerly of the main Shetland Isles. Another drive of some forty minutes took us to its northern tip, and the small car park on the edge of Hermaness National Nature Reserve.

An interpretation board at the gate showed the route of a circular path, about eight kilometres long, leading to the sea cliffs and so the puffins. As we loaded the camera gear into bags I noticed a disturbing shift in the weather. For most of our journey we had been travelling under clear skies and sunshine. Now, clouds rushed in from the west, dark and loaded with the threat of rain. I was going to regret missing that first ferry.

Undaunted, with everyone dressed for the potential down-pour, we set off up the winding footpath that led from the car park to the hills above. After about two hundred metres, Savannah was beginning to tire, and predictably was up and on my shoulders for the rest of the walk. The hike took us through moorland and bog, and through the terri-tories of one of the biggest great skua colonies on Shetland. I knew the bonxies could be aggressive at their nest sites, and stuck closely to the path where, I assumed, they would be used to seeing people walking and remain relaxed. With Savannah on my shoulders, she would be the highest point, and the first to be hit by any low-flying skua on a mission to dissuade us from entering its patch of ground. Once or twice birds flew by with a hint of malice in their body language, but none launched a dive-bombing raid, and soon we were through their colony and the tops of the sea cliffs were in view.

The cloud cover had deepened now and a chilly breeze had picked up. Keeping warm was not an issue for any of us, though: the effort of carrying the kit and Savannah over rough ground and up and down hills had me in a sweat, and Savannah was well dressed and clinging to a centrally heated dad.

It took the best part of an hour to reach the cliff tops, but the view once there made every sweaty step worthwhile. Swinging Savannah off my shoulders and dropping the heavy kit bag from my back, I joined Marguerite at the top of a gently sloping grass bank that led to the plunging sea cliffs.

'Not bad eh?' she said. 'Look, Babba, the sea.'

Our eyrie of a vantage point looked out over a vast sweep of jagged cliffs, the sea below the arena in a spectacular natural amphitheatre. In the distance, to the east, we could see rocky islands, whose tops appeared to be covered with snow. A closer inspection revealed the white caps to be a huge colony of gannets, their dense community blocking out the grey-black rock. Every ledge and crevice on the cliffs appeared to be occupied by one sea bird or another: fulmars near the tops, razorbills and guillemots further down. We found a fold in the ground that protected us from the wind and the three of us lay on our sides, Savannah tucked between us, to look out over the constantly shifting tableau. The distant seabirds were of vague interest to Savannah, but there was one much more accessible and confiding that we had come here to see, and we were not disappointed.

'Look there, what's that, Babba?' I whispered, pointing at the distinctive dumpy form of a nearby bird.

'PUFFIN!' Savannah knew the name from looking with me at bird books; even here, with the naked eye, the bird was close enough that its colours and character were instantly recognisable.

'MORE PUFFINS!' she squealed. Sure enough, as we scanned the grassy slope below us, it became apparent that they were everywhere, little clusters of birds standing together as though waiting for a bus.

'Stay close to us please, honey, the cliffs here are very, very high and we don't want to lose you.'

Savannah was excitedly wanting to get closer to the birds, but that would take her too near to the precipice, and though it was lovely to bring her with us to this rugged, wild place, I was nervous that she might run and lose her footing. We kept her tucked in close by our sides.

More puffins flew in from the sea and settled in front of us, each one a little closer than the last. Soon, we could all clearly see the colour and detail of the nearest birds with the naked eye. And then it started to rain. Not a downpour, but a light, steady drizzle from the west.

For many people, rain is the ruination of a day. Certainly it makes photography tricky, not least because keeping sensitive electronic equipment dry and in good working order is a challenge. Moisture on the lens renders shots unusable. Though we were equipped to film whatever we saw, the real purpose of the trip was to spend a solid day with our baby girl, and to share with her the spectacle and beauty of this northern outpost. Rain was not exactly welcome, but then neither was it enough to dampen our spirits. An oft-quoted snippet of wisdom came to mind: 'There's no such thing as bad weather, just the wrong clothes.' Fortunately we were all decked out in fine water-proofs, Savannah probably better equipped than any of us with her all-in-one insulated overall. We hunkered down with our backs to the breeze, rain dripping off our hoods and noses, and were very, very happy. At times the cloud came so low it partly obscured the cliffs before us, adding even greater scale and grandeur to the scene.

To say that happiness is a state of mind may seem blind-ingly obvious, but I find that many people veer towards a pessimistic slant on their lot in life and in so doing fulfil their fears of misery and gloom. Yes, it was raining, but we were warm, dry (on the inside), together in a huddle and in one of the most beautiful places on earth, surrounded by wild puffins that were now so obliging I could almost touch one or two of them. Nothing to complain about there!

Because I had delayed everyone by missing our ferry earlier, we had a very limited period that we could spend on the cliffs. The walk back would be physically challenging and lengthy, and we had to make the last ferry from Yell to Mainland if we were to sleep in our own beds tonight. After about an hour and a half at the cliffs, I reluctantly had to suggest that we should start the trek back to the car park.

Typically, as we walked down the final slope to our car,

the sun started to break through the clouds. By now Savannah was getting tired (though given that she was riding on my shoulders again, I'm not sure how much this had to do with her own physical exertion), and it was just as well we were going to start the journey home.

On the drive south through Unst, we passed by the most northerly bus stop in Britain. This is a modern affair, and could be an unremarkable structure were it not for the frivolous spirit of some local residents. I slowed as we neared the stop and pulled into a lay-by so that we could hop out and investigate.

Over several years, the drab, utilitarian interior of the shelter had been transformed by people with a sense of fun and quirky humour. I had seen it once before, in 2006, when it housed a sofa, coffee table, TV and standard lamp. Now, three years on, it had a pink theme. There was still a sofa (which in fact seemed to be a bank of old bus seats), covered in a pink fabric. Savannah thought this was terrific fun and ran into the shelter to explore. In a small bedside cupboard (pink, of course) she discovered a hoard of eclectic things, from a feather boa to a pink policewoman's hat (the fallout from a hen night, I suspected), and even a pink elephant cuddly toy. By now the sun was fully back out and the bus shelter was heating up, offering us an opportunity to warm up and dry out for five minutes before continuing our drive to the ferry terminal. Savannah had a ball, dancing around with the boa and beads around her neck and waving a pink feather duster like a wand. A telephone (not connected, of course) gave her endless fun, calling us to have a chat, despite the fact we were sitting next to her, and she spent a little while watching the TV, despite the fact it was not plugged in. If all this sounds a little surreal, it was. The singular sense of humour on show at the Baltasound bus shelter was a microcosm of all that I loved about people in Shetland; individual, quirky, light-hearted and prepared to invest huge effort in the pursuit of fun.

Not wanting to miss another ferry, I reluctantly had to ask Savannah to put all the bits back where she'd found them, so that the next folk to use the shelter would find everything in its place, and got back into the car to continue the drive south. Much as I had had fun in the bus shelter, I was surprised that Marguerite was finding it so enduringly amusing: she seemed unable to contain a giggle even when she had closed the car door and was buckling up.

'What's so funny?' I asked, a little bemused. Now Savannah started chuckling from her child-seat in the back.

'What? What is it?' I said, a bit miffed not to be in on the joke.

Marguerite stifled a laugh. 'Nothing . . . much,' and with that she let out a full-blown guffaw.

I looked at my reflection in the rear-view mirror.

'Very funny. Ha ha ha,' I said laconically. Unbeknownst to me, Marguerite had quietly placed the pink police-woman's hat on top of my usual peaked cap. I had no idea it was there and would have driven off wearing it, quite probably for the rest of the day, had she not started giggling. Hmmmmm.

On the road south, we passed by an old, brightly painted rowing boat on the side of the road, filled with earth and planted with a lovely display of flowers. Further illustration of the Unst eye for brightening up everyday objects.

We reached the southern ferry terminal at Belmont a good twenty minutes before the boat was due; time enough to explore the area around the car park. At first glance it was pretty spartan; a rock face backdrop which echoed to the guttural calls of a pair of fulmars, and a low wooden building housing the public loos. Slightly incongruous in this sombre, utilitarian landscape was a large billboard, on which a brightly coloured, abstract mural had been painted. It was eye-catching, if a little out of place, and I wandered over to it with Savannah. On the ground, just in front of the painting, was another large wooden rowing boat, which seemed like any other until you got close enough to look inside.

'Wow, Babba, come and look at this,' I urged, once I realised what had been created here.

Savannah stared wide-eyed at the ranks of metal pipes that were suspended with rough cord along the entire interior of the boat.

'Mummy, come and see.'

We all gathered around the biggest home-made xylophone any of us had ever seen. Indeed, this was the ONLY home-made xylophone any of us had ever seen. And what a creation! Metal pipes of different lengths and thickness were strung like the footboards of a rope bridge from one end of the boat to the other. Thoughtfully, some xylophone sticks had been left so that anyone waiting for the ferry – with time to kill and a musical bent – could strike away the minutes with chiming joy.

How completely, wonderfully, crazy, weird is that? Where else in the British Isles could you find a bus stop decorated like a pink boudoir and a boat that doubles as a public, outdoor xylophone? Unst is well known for its superlatives: Britain's most northerly post office, Britain's most northerly brewery (which incidentally makes some very fine ales). But not content with that, the community goes the extra mile to create something truly unique. And for nothing more than pure, unadulterated fun.

I lowered Savannah into the edge of the boat, and she happily chimed away the whole twenty minutes it took for the ferry to arrive. Peeling her away from the 'xyloboat', or 'rowaphone' was quite an ordeal, but we had to make our sailing connections to get back to the house before dark. The day had not been a resounding success on the filming front, but it couldn't have been a better way to share the magic of Shetland with our daughter.

We had to leave Shetland for the early part of the summer so that I could fulfil a commitment to the live TV series *Springwatch*. I was based in Wales for the whole of the transmission period, and though I was treated to some spectacular wildlife-watching, from goshawks to red kites and polecats, my mind often wandered to the wild shores further north and how the creatures there were faring. The moment I finished work on the live show, I was straight back up with my family, this time staying in another rented house in the east mainland.

# Chapter 16

## Simmer Dim

Having been away for the best part of a month, I was anxious to catch up with so many different wild characters it was hard to know where to start, but there was a date in the natural calendar that would not wait for weather, man or beast: the Simmer Dim, or longest days of summer.

Keen though I was to return, I was also mindful that we should ensure our arrival on the isles included the delicious period of acclimatisation afforded by the fourteen-hour ferry trip from Aberdeen to Lerwick. Coming in by plane might have been faster, but it didn't allow for our thoughts and energies to make the journey as sympathetically, and I chose to drive to Aberdeen from the south whilst Marguerite and Savannah flew; we met there before driving on to the ferry.

I noticed an unusually high number of leather-clad motorcyclists boarding at the same time as us, and was reminded that there was a rally held on Shetland each year, and had been almost every year since 1982, by bike enthusiasts keen to celebrate the longest day. I also discovered that the little house that we had rented was a mile or so from the fields where the hundreds of motorcyclists gathered, camped and made music to see in the turning point of the annual solar cycle.

On the evening of 21 June, we drove up to Eshaness in the northwest to film what proved to be an invisible sunset, shrouded with cloud and a light drizzle. The poor weather didn't inhibit the high spirits of the partying rally-goers, whose music and laughter we could hear coming up the hills when we got back to our house. I was sorry that neither they, nor we, were able to bask in the glory of an endless evening, but knew that before long there would be a break in the weather and that we would be there to enjoy it. A day or so after the weekend, my optimism proved well founded. We were now fully installed in our new rented house, the fields around were restored to calm now that the motorcyclists had started their return journeys south, and the clouds cleared. Midsummer is a time when all of life in Shetland is buzzing with energy. At midnight, with Savannah tucked up in bed, black plastic bin liners taped to her windows to stop the light in the sky from waking her, Marguerite and I walked to the hill behind the house to breathe in the atmosphere. We were presented with a magnificent scene.

The sky to the north was a deep, amber red, and its sister sea reflected the colour perfectly. The island of Yell rested with imposing grandeur as a dark, brooding mass to the north, its neighbouring smaller isles of Samphrey and Bigga peppering the ruby waters with their vivid silhouetted forms. There was not a breath of wind. The surface of the sea was so perfectly calm that each of the dark islands had transformed from low-lying slices of land to bulbous, ellipsoid masses, perfectly married to their reflections. There was sufficient light in the sky to read a book with ease, and the transit of the sun below the horizon was clearly marked by the more vivid red glow in the sky where it was hiding its face a few degrees out of view. Whilst the visual magnificence was breathtaking, it was the sounds of the Simmer Dim that set the hairs on my arms standing on end.

Every untamed voice that conjures up a sense of wilderness was there that night, each adding its contribution to the symphony with impeccable aesthetic timing. Snipe cut the air with their diving, drumming display flight. They plummeted towards the earth, stretching their corrugated outer tail feathers into the ripping air and producing their unearthly, vibrating, bleating percussion. It is a sound that is ventriloquial, colouring the night sky and at the same time seeming to be in your head. At the end of each diving flight, the birds rose up to gain height in preparation for the next dive, and as they did so they uttered a high, metronomic chirp, somewhat like a squeaking bicycle wheel. This was the percussion against which the other sounds of the Dim were painted. On the hills all around, golden plover fluted their mournful, bisyllabic piping calls. In keeping with the mood of the piece, their half-tones lent it a melancholic air. Now and then one would take flight in the gloom of distance, and shift its song into the more excited trilling phase. In my mind's eye, I could see them wavering over the dusky landscape, leaning this way and that before settling back next to their mate.

Next to offer its voice to the developing score was the curlew. If hills and moors could make a sound, this would be it. The curlew is not a songster; it cannot compete with a blackbird or nightingale for variety and complexity of tone. But in its simple, rich, woodwind of a call is held the spirit of wilderness. It reaches down into the heart of its ability and starts by delivering a repeated phrase that lifts from a low half-tone and slides seamlessly three notes higher. As its call grows in confidence, its voice begins to break, now a two-note refrain still in minor chords, sliding low to a high, wavering peak. This is often all that is heard; enough to paint the air with sufficient colour to satisfy the bird's and the human ear alike. But, from time to time, it will take its call to the next level and build to the crescendo, increasing the rhythm and pitch until the whole bird seems to be song, rising up an octave and adding vibrato and volume. If the start of the call is haunting and slightly sombre, then the climax is a magnificent, spine-tingling balance, full of energy, light, and almost literally bubbling with joy. As the first of the curlew reached this peak in this endless gloaming, my every nerve end tingled and I experienced a flush of pure joy. Other voices now rose up from the shoreline below the house, so far away it seemed impossible that they could reach my ears. But the air was so profoundly still and the amphitheatre effect of the bay and hills around me so acoustically efficient, I was perfectly positioned to pick up every detail.

Dunlin added their trilling display calls and then, from the fields below the house, a song I had not heard for many years rose up from the hay meadow. It was once the sound of agricultural Britain in summer, before the days of intensive farming methods, where grass is now turned into silage rather than allowed to grow through the early summer and be cut as hay as a winter feed for livestock. Millions of acres of rural Britain are now farmed with such ruthless efficiency that there is no room for any herbs, insects or the birds that depend on them.

'Wet my lips – wet my lips – wet my lips . . .' The phonetic mnemonic that describes the song of the quail bounced up the hill to the crest where I stood. I felt a flush of excitement, and wondered for a moment if this was a vagrant rarity, so far north. I then remembered that Shetland was on the northern limit of the European quail's global distribution, and that its almost mechanical song was very much a part of summers here in the past. Due to the land-use changes both here in its breeding grounds and perhaps in North Africa where, remarkably for a small, dumpy, short-winged game bird, it spends the winter, numbers everywhere in Britain have crashed. Thirty years ago, I used to hear them calling in meadows on the Somerset Levels and from fields on the Mendip Hills. As far as I am aware, it has been years since their bouncing song has brightened the summer days in that part of their former range. Depending on the year, anything from a handful to just over 300 males may now sing on our shores; this adventurous pioneer of the far north I was hearing was hoping to sing down a female from the night sky. The chances of him finding a mate were slim, but I hoped that his efforts and optimism would be rewarded.

Whilst I revelled in the myriad voices around me, there was one missing that I longed to hear. I wondered if perhaps I was too far from any hill loch to be within earshot of my favourite of all Shetland bird calls, but I should have known better. They simply had impeccable theatrical timing.

A lull in the general avian conversation seemed to give them their cue. Far in the distance, a red-throated diver started its drawn-out wailing. It was as if the very soul of the Simmer Dim were speaking, hurling the agonies and the ecstasies of the year gone by to the hills. Every hair on my body (and I still have a few, despite appearances) was electrified. The catlike calls tumbled down from the high ground and climaxed in a duet, with both members of a pair rolling their chorus one on top of the other. They were joined by the voices of curlew, plover and quail.

Never was there a more hauntingly lovely natural soundscape.

The next day, after very little sleep, I was on a mission. There was a bird whose natural calendar coincided with our return and warranted immediate attention.

The last time I had watched red-necked phalaropes was in 2006 with the *Springwatch* team, and I dearly wanted to revisit and film their quirky breeding antics. Fortunately, they are the latest of the breeding summer migrants to arrive in Shetland, many not turning up on the isles until June, and the females still busily chatting up the uncommitted males in the middle and end of the month. I had been in contact with Malcie Smith and Martha of the RSPB, and had organised the relevant licences and permissions to work with this rarest of birds. Malkie had informed me that numbers had been stable over the past three years, but that still left only about forty males in the whole of Britain, ninety per cent of which were found in Shetland.

I travelled to the North Isles on the morning of a spectacularly lovely day. The ferry trips were conducted on ice-smooth seas and the early yellow light suffused the passing terns and gulls with an ochre tint. By the time I met with Malkie, it was already late morning, and having pored over maps and discussed tactics, we headed out for one of the island's most famous venues for phalaropes, Loch Funzie. This large freshwater loch, (pronounced 'Finny') is part of an RSPB reserve and well known for its phalaropes. We checked the shallow waters around the shoreline with our binoculars and spotted at least two females working through the emergent sedges on the far side.

'This should do the trick, thank you, Malcie,' I said, whilst I prepared the camera kit for filming. The loch and some of the surrounding small pools attracted birds from a few breeding spots in the vicinity, and it wasn't long before the first of them was whirring to within a few metres of where I now sat on the edge of the pool. As the afternoon made its gentle sweep into evening, the quality of light intensified and other birds came to visit the loch. Arctic skuas, pirates of the bird world, flew in to drink and bathe, and were joined by their bigger cousins, the bonxies. Terns fished over the loch's centre, and red-throated divers, which nested nearby, drifted out on to the water from time to time to snooze or occasionally preen and bathe.

By seven in the evening, the air was still dead calm, and the temperature easing back from a high of the mid-twenties; a remarkable summer's day this far north. The female phalaropes present on the loch became suddenly animated at the sight of a male coming to the water to feed. He was almost certainly incubating a clutch of eggs on a nest nearby and, since he was alone in the nesting duties, wanted only to rapidly satisfy his hunger and get back to incubate his brood. This did not deter the four emancipated females from trying to make a pass at him, and they twittered and fussed in his path as he feverishly pecked at tiny flies on the surface.

After some animated squabbling, one of the females seemed to shadow him more calmly and closely, and I assumed she was what might loosely be called his mate. Though she would not help with rearing the family any more, she did have a vested interest in preventing other females getting involved with the male she had entrusted her genetic future to. He, meanwhile, benefited from her protection, because now he could concentrate on feeding whilst she kept the other females from bothering him. It seemed like a good deal all round, though I knew that the mother of his brood could not be trusted to stick around for the whole season. She might well look for another male to lay more eggs with, and was likely to leave Shetland long before her chicks were fledged. For now, though, the pair swam alongside each other, the ever-deepening saffron light enriching the colours of the female still further and making the landscape glow a saturated orange. I watched the birds, bathed in the late warmth of the summer sun, and allowed my imagination to be carried by the sounds of dunlin, whimbrel and snipe calling and displaying all around me. I had one of my moments. I know I should avoid dangerously mawkish eulogies about being happy in a wild environment, but there are times you just have to come clean; to accept that you are a hopeless nerd and are completely in love with what you do. This was one of those moments!

# Chapter 17

## Seabirds and Silicon Chips

The summer of 2009 will go down in Shetland history as one of the finest on record. Whilst counties in southern England were getting drenched and chilled by unseasonal rain, we were enjoying day after day of unbroken sunshine, warmth and calm. No one dared talk too much about it lest it cast a jinx on the run of fair skies, but everyone enjoyed it, and Marguerite and I could make the most of every one of the long hours of daylight available to us, following the islands' wildlife. Because we had been so fortunate with the weather, we felt justified in taking an afternoon off to visit Lerwick during the weekend of the Flavour of Shetland festival.

Now in its fourth year, the festival was a relatively new addition to the calendar of events taking place on the isles, but was nonetheless hugely popular. The weekend included an eclectic mix of music, stalls featuring local food produce, crafts and culture, and was a welcome change for us after all the time we had spent alone in the field with wildlife. Savannah surprised me once again by standing as close as she could to the main stage to dance to music performed by a mix of folk and rock artists. I thought she might be daunted by the volume and energy of it all, but not a bit of it! We met with Helen Moncrieff and, as well as enjoying the food and drink, had a chance to catch up and discuss plans to film on the island of Mousa and later at Sumburgh Head. I was also flattered to be asked by Helen – and I readily agreed – to give a talk at the Shetland Nature Festival which was coming up in July. It was the very least I could do after all the tremendous help we had been given by so many people.

After a great day enjoying the celebration of all things Shetland, we were back on track, making the most of the fair weather for filming. It had been some time since we checked the remote cameras trained on the gannet nest on Noss, and I wanted to make at least one more trip to the island to see if the pair we had been following had successfully hatched a chick. With the forecast showing a huge high nestled over the isles, we decided to make a full day of it, taking Savannah along with us, to enjoy the sun and sea.

The crossing to Noss in the little inflatable was smooth and easy and, once we had regrouped with all the gear and supplies necessary for the day, Marguerite, Savannah and I struck out on the long walk to the cliffs. Savannah got about four hundred metres before complaining that she was tired, and asking whether she could go on my shoulders. My pleasure.

I had already worked up a head of steam carrying all the camera gear. Now, with Savannah nestled on my shoulders and backpack, I would have a proper work out! She was delighted, singing tunes from *The Sound of Music* and bouncing happily up and down in time with her rhythm. Her wobbling didn't make the going any easier for me, nor did her new-found joke of covering my eyes with her hands as we approached difficult terrain or cliff ledges. I saw the funny side of it, when I could see anything at all! Along the way we realised too late that we had wandered into the nesting territory of a great black-backed gull, when the adult bird came swooping low at our heads, screaming insults at the intruders. Savannah thought this terribly funny.

'Silly bird, Daddy,' she chuckled. I knew that if the gull decided to drive home its attack, she would be rather less amused. The gulls have the capacity to give you a nasty whack with their lowered feet as they whizz past your head, and Savannah, being the highest point, would be the first to get hit. We moved away quickly, pausing only briefly to take a peek at the fluffy gull chick huddled in the grass nearby.

The rest of the long walk to the cliffs took it out of our daughter, despite the fact she wasn't doing any of the walking. By the time we reached the Noup, she had fallen fast asleep, her head resting on mine, her dead weight giving me some interesting balancing challenges as I negotiated the rougher ground on the approach.

She grizzled a bit as I lay her on Marguerite's coat, but settled back into a snooze whilst we prepared the camera gear and monitoring device needed to check the remote camera feeds. By the time we were ready to plug the first of the camera cables in to the little screen, Savannah was wide awake and back to her usual jolly self. She remembered how to set up the monitor and cameras from our watching the oystercatcher nest in the spring, and it was she that plugged the first camera in to the set-up and looked at the screen.

'It's not working, Daddy,' she said, looking hard at the monitor.

'Are you sure honey? Let's have another go,' I said, assuming she had not plugged the system together properly. I should not have doubted her. The wires were all in good order but, as she rightly observed, there was nothing coming from the camera that looked horizontally at the nest.

'Oh dear. It's broken,' I said, rather fatuously given that my two-and-a-half-year-old daughter had already made the same observation.

I was disappointed but, of the two cameras fixed on the nest, this was the least valuable view given that it had already suffered severe water ingress earlier in the year. I assumed it was this that had finally prevented it from working at all, and prepared to plug in the cable from the camera looking down at the nest. Savannah stared at the screen as the connection was made.

'Birds, Daddy!'

Ah, now at least we had something. Marguerite and I lay on the ground next to Savannah and shielded the screen from the glare of the sun. There had unfortunately been further moisture or salt spray on the lens port of the camera housing, but the view was clear enough to see that all seemed to be well on the nest, with an adult bird sitting tight in the centre of frame. It was also sufficiently clear to see what had happened to the other camera, which had once offered the side view. From time to time, a length of black cable swung into view, the end broken and frayed. I assumed that the birds had indulged in a bout of enthusiastic nest-material collection, and one of the gannets had taken a shine to the cable as a potential addition to its structure. The bill of a gannet is strong and sharp enough to grip a large slippery fish like a mackerel, so snipping through the wire would have been easy for it. We had secured the cable to the rock face with numerous ties back in February, hoping to keep it out of reach. But I guess if you are used to flying over the ocean and plunge diving after fish, then hours spent sitting on a nest must get a little tedious after a while, and the opportunity to solve a simple problem like, 'How can I rip that black shiny rope from the wall?', would be hard to resist. The gannets had all the time in the world to work out a way of getting the cable off the cliff face, and had clearly done just that.

The feed from the one remaining camera grew progressively better the longer it was left on, and after half an hour we had a pretty good view of proceedings on the nest. It was very hard to see what was going on under the sitting bird until its mate returned with a scrap of nest material as a coming-home gift and both parents stood to clatter beaks and preen each other. There, nestled at the feet of the adult female, was a fluffy white chick. The fact that it was already covered in down meant that it was at least a week and a half old. When gannets first emerge from the egg they are virtually naked, a blackish scrap of flesh with a disproportionately large beak.

'Look, Babba, they've got their chick, and we've got our

chick,' I said, giving Savannah a hug. I could forgive the relatively poor output of the camera for the super-intimate view it afforded us of the activity at the nest. It had taken some serious effort and manpower to sneak a peek into the private life of 'our' pair, but from my point of view it had been worth it.

We spent the rest of the afternoon filming more conventional views of the colony and sitting with Savannah amongst the very accommodating puffins opposite the Holm of Noss, and by early evening we were sunbeaten, tired and happy. The walk back to the small ferry crossing point at Gungstie on the west of the island was again too much to ask of Savannah and she rode the journey out on my shoulders, falling asleep once more and flopping on to my head. Despite the extra weight, I loved having my little girl draped over my shoulders as we worked our way back down the hill to meet the warden who would take us across to Bressay and our car. My shoulders didn't love it the following day, though: they ached as if I had done a thousand press-ups.

Having satisfied my ambition at the gannet nests, there was another feature of our biggest seabird's life that I wanted to reveal. Gannets are consummate fishermen, plunge diving from about ten metres and hitting the water at speeds in excess of a hundred kilometres an hour. The precision, power and grace of the act makes for an awesome sight when you witness a single bird doing it. If a flock gathers to plunder a large shoal of fish, the resulting show ranks among the greatest natural spectacles on earth.

Because of their speed, it is very difficult to fully appreciate the subtleties of the birds' astonishing abilities with the naked eye, and I hoped to be able to record gannets diving using a super-slow-motion camera.

The equipment was rented and shipped to the islands in the hope that the weather would hold and we would have an opportunity to record the gannets whilst the pressure for them to find food to satisfy the appetite of their growing chicks was at its highest.

I had used this digital high-speed camera before to film a number of high-octane natural events, from cheetahs chasing gazelles in Kenya's Masai Mara, to great white sharks leaping to catch fur seals in South Africa. In the UK I had filmed ospreys, red kites and goshawks with it, but this was the first time I'd had the chance to try it with gannets.

I had recorded gannets diving in slow motion once before, for the series *The Blue Planet*, many years earlier. At the time, high-speed digital film cameras were not of a high enough quality to be broadcast and we were still shooting on sixteen-millimetre film stock. The camera I was using had a maximum speed of four hundred and fifty frames a second, slowing the action by eighteen times. The faster the frame rate, the shorter the time each frame of film was exposed to the image, and with film stocks being of limited light sensitivity, we had to have direct and brilliant sunshine to run the camera on the action at full speed. The location then was the waters around the Bass Rock off the Scottish east coast, where eighty thousand gannets breed annually. It was August

1999 and the remit for the shoot was quite straightfor-ward. Film the birds diving. Can't get simpler than that! As it turned out, though, the weather conditions conspired to make it very difficult indeed. The shots had to be achieved from a boat to get the desired angle and prox-imity to the action, but the sea state simply did not allow us to film for days on end. Each morning we made our way to the little port at North Berwick, looked out at the ocean being churned by high winds and returned, frus-trated, to the hotel.

On the morning of 11 August, it looked, at last, as though everything was going to come together. The wind had dropped to a slightly eerie whisper, the sun was shining and we headed out full of hope and expectation that this was the day. We reached the rock a little before ten in the morning and offered the gannets a few herring from the crates we had brought along. Within a few minutes we had a good flock gathering and I prepared to film, settling low on a dive platform at the back of the boat to maximise the impact of the view. And then something strange started to happen. The sun began to go out. At first I could not understand how, on such a lovely cloudless day, the later it got in the morning, the darker was the sky. It grew cold, too, and I got back on to the deck of the boat, unable to run the camera at a high frame rate in this gloom. And then it clicked. The solar eclipse. For the first time in seventy years, Britain was in the path of a total eclipse of the sun. Where we were, about eighty per cent of the sun was covered, quite enough to make it feel and look like dusk. The gannets started to head back to the island, confused and thinking about an early night, and I must have been one of the very few people in the UK quietly cursing my luck.

Now, ten years on, I wanted to make sure no unforeseen problems could arise to scupper our chances of filming the birds at their most dynamic. The new generation of slow-motion cameras no longer used film but instead recorded images as files in a computer. What made these instruments exceptional is that we could now record up to almost a million and a half frames per second! Some of the old laws of photography still applied, though: the faster the frame rate, the more light required to get a good image, and there was a certain law of sod which would inevitably rear its ugly head if we weren't careful.

With Marguerite, I started to set up the camera to run a couple of shots of something predictably fast moving (which turned out to be Marguerite jumping up and down on the spot). I just wanted to test the system before using it in earnest, but, as it turned out, I didn't even get that far. Because the camera I was using was really designed for studio applications where mains electricity is available, I had to have a number of bespoke items made before it could be efficiently used in the field. These included batteries and cables to run a viewfinder for protracted periods. As I plugged the viewfinder into its power source, there was an unpleasant electronic popping sound, and I immediately knew something very wrong had happened. I checked the system carefully and discovered to my horror that the battery cable had been wired with reverse polarity. At least I knew why the viewfinder had blown up, but I had no idea how to fix it. In all honesty, I doubted very much that I would find anyone on Shetland who did, knowing how tricky these complex bits of electronic wizardry can be to repair. We tested the rest of the system as best we could, but though I could record slow-motion images without the viewfinder, there was no way I could follow the fast-moving action of diving gannets without a direct feed of the visual information to my eye.

I was crestfallen. The weather was still holding fair but for how much longer? I am usually a very positive person – at least, I like to think so (Ha) – but I really did think perhaps my attempts to film gannets diving would be forever destined to be an uphill struggle. I phoned friends on the islands, and asked who they thought might be able to help. The same name came up on several occasions: Last Ditchology in Lerwick.

I discovered that the facility was run as part of a company with charitable status called COPE (Community Opportunities for Participation in Enterprise), which gave adults with disabilities the opportunity to take part in meaningful, productive and developing enterprise. They had several fabulous success stories to their name, including a sandwich and soap-making business, and Last Ditchology was allied to the Shetland Scrap Store, a business that recycled furniture. With a similar will to keep electronic equipment alive and well, the engineers at Last Ditchology fixed everything from record players to toasters, striving to reduce the culture of waste so many of us are guilty of indulging. I had nothing but admiration for the principles at the heart of both COPE and the industries it encouraged, but I truly doubted that they would be able to respond to my very niche request.

I arrived at the given address in a business park on the edge of town and found a small wooden shed, tucked at the end of the car park, brandishing the business name. Davy and Brian, the engineers, greeted me cautiously as I stuck my head in the door and warned me that they were just preparing to close shop for the day. I explained my predicament and asked when they might be able to take a look at the broken viewfinder.

'Bring us it in here now, and we'll have a look,' Davy offered generously.

I explained what the cause of the failure had been, and he and Brian immediately rattled off a number of likely problems the unit would have suffered through being wired incorrectly. None sounded very good.

'Let's get it open and have a look inside then,' Davy said as he reached for a screwdriver. Matters were made worse when we realised that this piece of equipment had been treated somewhat roughly in the past and, where screws should have been holding it together, lashings of glue had been applied.

At this, Davy reached for a much bigger screwdriver and a large drill. I dared not watch as he set to the task of getting the thing open, and could only imagine the rental company's reaction if they knew what was going on with their precision instrument.

At one point he quipped that he had a Kango hammer in the car, used for breaking cement, should we have any more trouble.

'That's got it,' he declared as the viewfinder eventually gave up in the face of dogged perseverance and split in two.

'Now then, let's see what we have here . . . Aha! There's the problem.'

Davy reached inside the guts of fine wires, printed circuits, resistors and diodes, and pulled out a tiny black component that had several hair-thin wires coming from it.

'There, you can see where it's blown.'

I can tell the difference between a marsh tit and a willow tit, but I struggle with electronic components. I couldn't see what made this tiny blob of resin in the least bit suspect until Davy fished around inside the cavity of the viewfinder again and brought out an even smaller shard of resin that fitted an irregular corner of the component.

'Blown it clean apart. That's finished, no chance we'll mend that.'

I was grateful to the chaps for taking the time to look, and prepared to leave.

'Hang on, we've not finished yet.' Davy studied the faulty item through a magnifying glass, then called out a serial number to Brian.

'We'll not have that one, but we may have something like it.' Brian muttered as he went to a bank of tiny plastic drawers mounted on the wall at the back of the shed. The two men had entered the world of engineering that I find close to alchemy. They spoke of resistors, capacitors, inductors, suppressors and, as far as I could tell, conductors, though I may have misheard the latter; they seemed lost in a world of their own for a moment.

'Here, try this one.' Brian eventually settled on a thingy

that looked exactly like the other thingy from the viewfinder, but without the little shard missing.

After some astonishingly precise soldering, which amounted to joining hair-like wires to a pinhead, Davy stepped away from the bench.

'Right then. Let's fire it up and see what we've done to it,' he said with a mischievous smile.

I had everything crossed as power and a video feed was applied to the viewfinder. At first nothing, then it flick-ered into life.

'We have a picture . . . YES!' I yelled. 'Thank you so much, guys, you are complete stars. What do I owe you?'

'Nothing, we do this one for free.' I thought they were kidding at first, but the whole ethos of the business was to make money through selling repaired items, but to offer a service to the community as well, by fixing things that had gone wrong for a small fee, and free to charitable groups and such like. I was humbled and speechless.

Savannah, camera operator extraordinaire. Then she wiped her nose on the lens!

Marguerite and me not posing at all.

The cliffs at Sumburgh. The guillemot colonies stain the rocks white with
their droppings. I'm just visible on top of the cliff by the wall.

Guillemot adults and a chick. He could jump at any moment!

The father leads his chick off to Norway. Phew!

The islands are connected with regular ferry services.

Why waste letters?

Filling up at rush hour.

Distant horizons and room to think.

Marguerite and Savannah after a major daisy picking session.

Sand dolphins on a 'secret' beach. Savannah and me.

The emancipated lady. Red-necked phalarope.

The simmer dim.

Just the beginning.

# Chapter 18

## Loss and Gain

With all the stars lining up now, shining positively on my ambition to film the gannets in slow motion, I didn't expect the phone call from Jan. Kirikoo had died.

Jan wanted to tell me personally the moment she knew, but was too upset to contact me right away. After managing to compose herself, she made the call, and I received the news parked in a bleak lay-by on the way back from Lerwick. The exact cause of death was uncertain. Kirikoo had all that she needed: food, water, shade and shelter. She had just given up. Perhaps it was a viral infection; perhaps it was a lingering nerve injury that finally took its toll. Jan, naturally, soul-searched for answers that were hard to come by.

I found the passing of the little otter deeply upsetting – strangely so, given that I had only met her on a few occasions; though fond of her, I was, I thought, pragmatic about her chances of long-term survival. But her death struck a chord in me that echoed losses I had suffered in the past with other creatures I had nurtured and invested love and care in, notably an orphaned cheetah cub called Sambu. I had helped care for him and his brother Toki, in Lewa Wildlife Conservancy in northern Kenya, with a view to reintroducing them to the wild. Over two years, we stayed with the boys by day, and, once they were living wild, through the night whenever we were in Kenya. Both had been living free for months when Sambu was unexpectedly and shockingly killed by a lion.

That incident affected me, and all who worked with the cheetah brothers, profoundly.

I now found myself empathising deeply with Jan's grief; the phases of loss that inevitably play over and over in your head when you have been caring for a creature; the self-examination; the probing for answers that would never come.

Perhaps Kirikoo's passing was a blessing, a release for the little creature whose instinct and entire being compelled it to run and swim and dive, things it quite probably would never be able to do. Recently she had shown no sign of improvement, and if anything the paralysis of her hindquarters had been getting worse, despite constant physiotherapy and care.

An impossible decision about her future had been made by fate and circumstance. But however 'right', however rational, it was not easy to accept, especially for Jan and Pete. I promised I would visit them soon and hung up, left with my thoughts, letting them stray across the bay below and towards the horizon.

The sombre mood was lifted by the promise of another day of sunshine and calm, and the prospect of a very exciting mission.

We had been in touch with Tom Jamieson, who runs the Mousa Ferry, and chartered his boat to try and film the gannets diving. He had procured several boxes of locally caught mackerel the night before, as incentive for the birds to plunge on to the water close to the boat, and we left the little slipway at Sandsayre full of hope and the promise of a good day at sea. The digital high-speed camera was working (or it least it had been the last time I checked), the sea was near flat calm, the sun was shining and warm. What could possibly go wrong?

As we left the harbour I noticed a couple of gannets flying high overhead and wondered if we could attract them within range of the camera by throwing a couple of fish in the water. No sooner had we done so than gulls appeared from nowhere, herring and great black-backed, and within minutes we were surrounded by a flock of more than fifty, squawking and harrying by the boat, hoping for a free meal. The gannets did check their flight and circle high overhead, but with such a barrage of gull bodies in the way, they seemed reluctant to commit to a dive and flew on without even attempting to grab one of the fish I had proffered.

So, it wasn't going to be that easy. Calling on my experiences from the Bass Rock years earlier (and having checked that there was no solar eclipse forecast), I chatted to Tom about the possibility of sailing closer to Noss where the main colony on the east coast was based. He readily agreed and we set the throttle to full, heading for the island ten miles or so to the north. The journey gave me time to prepare the camera with Marguerite and refine our proposed strategy should we be lucky enough to attract any birds.

We reached the southern tip of Noss after forty minutes

or so and slowed the engines, keeping a reasonable distance from the breeding cliffs. Though I hoped to attract gannets, I wanted to ensure there was a choice of backdrop too, from the dark shadow of the cliffs to the open sea. As I prepared to throw the first fish into the water, a shiver of excitement ran down my spine. This was the moment of truth. Within seconds of the fish hitting the surface, two or three gannets that had been patrolling overhead checked their flight and plunged towards the surface. The fastest among them plummeted into the sea and came up with its prize. It was going to work!

With Tom manning the boat and taking charge of fish distribution and Marguerite and I priming the camera gear, we were in a position to start filming.

'Throw them in just in front of me here please, Tom; just a couple of metres away would be great,' I called as I put my eye to the now fully functioning eyepiece and prepared to frame up on the action. At the other end of the cables running from the camera, Marguerite was hunched over a laptop computer, jacket over her head to exclude the sunlight from the screen, checking the system parameters and preparing to press the start button. The camera could be triggered from a remote switch or the computer, and I plumped for the latter, needing both hands to manipulate framing and focus and sitting close enough to Marguerite to yell 'Fire' when necessary.

With four or five fish in the water, the excitement among the birds, and us humans, was tangible. The guttural, raucous calls of gannets overhead grew louder, and the shadows cast by their long pointed wings flickered over the deck with Hitchcockian portent. And then they came, sudden spears of white feather and flesh bolting into the water before me, the impact sounding like a dull explosion, three or four at a time all vying for the same fish.

'More fish please, Tom,' I yelled above their calls.

More and more gannets arrived, drawn by the sight of their fellow fishermen plunging into the sea.

'FIRE!' I called as a bird belted into frame directly in front of me. Marguerite pressed the trigger button and called back.

'Got it! Let's have a look.'

One huge advantage of the digital image over film was about to be put to the test. Where in the past, when filming gannets at the Bass Rock, I had to wait for days before any film footage was processed so that I could assess its quality, now we could have an instant replay of the action. I had set the camera to record at five hundred frames per second. This effectively slows the movement of a recorded subject by twenty times, since the image is replayed at twenty-five frames per second. The action in the image was lovely, the detail of the bird's preparation to enter the water graphic and revealing.

'Let's have another go, numbers are really building now,' I suggested. Before we could reset the camera and prepare it for another shot, we had to save the existing image to memory. This was the downside of the system. In the past, when using it to film other unpredictable events, I had been halfway through the long-winded saving process and been unable to react to something equally or more spectacular taking place before me, simply because the computer was tied up. This was especially true when working with the sharks in South Africa. The gannets were at least a little more predictable and I thought we should have several opportunities to record their action, given that they were waiting for us to offer them a fish.

With the first of the shots 'stuck to memory', we continued to try and improve on the views we were recording. The light was as good as it gets and I wound the frame rate up to one thousand frames per second, slowing the action forty times. The results were simply wonderful, but it was the natural event that really made the adrenalin flow. When you are surrounded by gannets plunging into the water at full speed, it is an exhilarating experience by anyone's standards. The sounds are over-whelming, the visual impact astonishing. But, it is very hard to see what is really going on. By slowing the action down so dramatically, the performance takes on a dream-like quality, a whole new aesthetic, but also allows you to analyse the dive in minute detail.

A foraging bird circles or flies slowly over the sea at a height of about fifteen metres. All the time, it scours the water below, using its binocular vision which can stare down past its substantial beak, to pick up the tiniest clue that a fish is moving close enough to the surface to be a viable target. It may be that their eyes have polarizing qualities to help spot prey through the reflected glare of the surface. When it does see a fish, the bird reacts imme-diately, often pivoting on one wing and shifting and realigning its approach dive throughout the vertical drop. Just before they hit the water they may be travelling at speeds of over a hundred kilometres per hour, a neck-breaking pace, one might think. But just before it pierces the surface, several unique adaptations come into play, many of which were now graphically revealed by the ultra-slow-motion images we were getting. With the eyes and head focused on the quarry, the wings are brought back in a long elegant sweep along the body. If you tried to force the wings of, say, an eagle into the same position, they would break at the shoulder joint. The head, wings and body now take on a near perfect arrow shape, fired – as it were – from the bow-like arch of the bird prior to the dive, a feature which led to their old Cornish name of *Saithor*, meaning arrow.

Hitting the water at such speed could rip a bird in two if it were not perfectly aligned. The tip of the beak pierces the meniscus, opening the way for the rest of the bird to follow. The gannet has no external nostrils so the tremendous force of water cannot shoot up its nose. The skull is reinforced on the forehead and around the eye sockets, as are the vertebrae in the neck, all to withstand the force of impact. There is surprisingly little splash created by the dive, so beautifully streamlined is the bird's form, but the footage revealed that by the time any impact splash had truly developed, the gannet was already a long way under water and closing in on its target.

Because we were offering dead fish, the birds did not have to plunge to great depths, nor perform rapid manoeuvres to grab their meal, but in the open sea and targeting a shoal of herring or mackerel, they reach between fourteen and thirty-four metres below the surface, the initial part of the dive aided by the momentum of the stoop, and the remainder of the dive in pursuit of a fleeing fish assisted by paddling with their broad, webbed feet.

'Awesome Tom, really great!' I called over the wall of gannet voices. 'Just another couple of shots and I think we're there.'

We were all on a high. Having hundreds of the nation's biggest seabirds circling overhead and knowing that our mission had been all but achieved was a great feeling. But even better was taking a moment to look away from the camera and marvel at the unadulterated beauty of it all. The great dark cliffs behind, which I knew were home to our growing gannet chick on the nest with the remote cameras, the perfectly blue sky, Marguerite concentrating on downloading the most recently shot images to the computer hard drive, the birds overhead. There are moments in life you want to hold forever, and this was one.

With enough material to ensure we had a strong sequence of gannet behaviour secured on the computer hard drive, we headed south to the harbour at Sandsayre. We still had a couple of crates of fish remaining, and I felt that the very least we could do was offer them to the gannets that had provided us with such an extraordinary natural spectacle. I tossed them over the stern one by one, and the birds followed, a great stream of white against the cobalt sky, like the steam from the funnel of an ocean liner. A relay of plunging forms followed the fish I cast overboard, and where they had left the trail, others took their place, hopeful of success with the next offering. There must have been in excess

of five hundred gannets following the boat and a smattering of gulls, some of which cheekily cadged a lift on
the rail at the stern.

With the last of the fish in the water, our entourage
thinned, then waned, and we were left with only a couple
of herring gulls, hoping that some scraps might be left
for their patience. I tossed them the remaining dregs from
the bottom of the fish crate and we made the rest of the
journey back to harbour without any followers. It had
been a curious couple of days, the lows of losing the little
otter and the broken equipment tempered by the all-time
high of the gannet extravaganza. Life and death, fortune
and misfortune: a perfect, if sobering balance.

The summer rush to raise a family before the onset of
the darker days to come was in full swing now. As well
as the gannets, other seabirds – razorbills, fulmars, black
guillemots, kittiwakes and many more – were all working
hard to find sufficient food to satisfy the appetite of their
new families as well as to ensure the adults would stay
fit. This annual peak in demand for fish has been a major
problem with the seabird populations in Shetland in the
recent past. In the 1980s and early 1990s there was a
dramatic decline in the number of breeding pairs of many
species, and in some years the success rate of birds that
did nest was zero in some colonies. The reasons for such
a crash in numbers are undoubtedly multiple, but the
evidence suggests that the single most important factor
in seabird breeding success is availability of food. For
many, the food in question are sand eels: small, narrow

silver fish that shoal in their thousands during the summer months. Or should.

Until recently, Shetland and other fishing communities, notably Denmark, had a thriving industry based on sand eels. Many tons were taken from the ocean each year and used in everything from fish food pellets to support the salmon farming industry, to fishmeal in fertiliser and pig food, and oil for margarine. With huge pressure on stocks (the Shetland stock not being self sustaining) it was inevitable that the population would, sooner or later, collapse. Between 1991 and 1994, there was a ban on all sand-eel fishing in Shetland waters, as a direct response to the cataclysmic drop in seabird breeding success. Recovery for a population of fish after such indiscriminate and prolonged attack is slow. Years after the ban, seabirds were still struggling, and many are to this day. The breeding success of arctic terns in 2008, when we started our adventures in Shetland, was terribly low. But in 2009 it looked as though things might have turned a corner. Wherever I looked – in small bays, or out on the open sea – flocks of terns, accompanied by raiding skuas and the occasional gannet, fluttered over the ocean and plunged repeatedly down to take fish from close to the surface. A close look revealed sand eels in their beaks. It is impossible to speculate just how well the sand-eel stocks might have recovered. It could have been an unusual shift of shoals from the south around Orkney that was responsible for the sudden glut, or a brief peak in a population that would later waver and crash once more. But all the signs were good. Numbers of terns returning to traditional colonies were the highest they had been for many years. Guillemots and razorbills came back regularly to the nest with the little silver fish in their bills, ready to offer them to their chicks. If things continued this way, then we were cautiously looking at the best breeding season for seabirds in Shetland for many years.

Among the many species whose lives were inextricably linked with the sand-eel stocks were puffins. The fish are undoubtedly the prey item of choice for a puffin feeding its chick; the species in the clichéd image of a puffin with its beak stuffed with fish will almost invariably be sand eels. Puffins are, in fact, one of the few seabirds still able to raise a chick when sand-eel stocks are low. Unlike terns and kittiwakes, they can dive to extraordinary depths to search for prey, and so have a wider choice available than some others, whose shallow dives can only penetrate to within a few centimetres of the surface. Only sand eels regularly swim in that upper column of water in any numbers. There is no doubt, though, that when sand eels are available, they are the food of choice for puffins too.

After spending time earlier in the year preparing some potential puffin burrows at Sumburgh Head for filming the hidden interior, it was time to return and check to see if any had been occupied.

I had prepared a nest-checking device, taping a little camera to a stick and some Christmas tree lights alongside it to illuminate the gloom of the burrow. Marguerite and I joined Helen at Sumburgh with all the gear, and with a big dollop of optimism. We scrabbled down the slope on the north face of the point to the first of the prepared burrows. It took a while to find the right holes in the ground, now that the grass had grown, but we eventually found the first of the old rabbit burrows that we had adapted with plastic pluming to receive the cameras and lights. I carefully pushed the probe into the burrow, and studied the little screen we had brought to show us its output. I was a little nervous that there might be an adult bird within, perhaps sitting on an egg still, and that our intrusion might upset it, but, as it turned out, the only visible life at the end of the burrow was a large black slug.

'Oh well, one down, one thousand nine hundred and ninety nine to go,' I smiled to Helen as I pulled the camera out of the burrow and prepared to check the next one. We worked our way systematically across the upper slopes of the cliff, checking each burrow we had rigged with pipes, and some that we had not yet adapted. Often the burrow was too twisted for us to be sure of its contents, and others were just too long. We did find puffin chicks in a few, balls of black fluff with an afterthought of a beak stuck on the top, huddled at the back of the chambers. But for one reason or another, whether it was too many rocks in the way, or too steep a curve to the burrow, none were ideal for filming.

We started back up the slope, aiming to check burrows on the north side of the point, which had also been prepared earlier in the year to receive a mini camera, when I passed a burrow I thought I recognised.

'Hey Helen, remember this one?' I called across to where she was peering into another burrow. 'I think this is the tunnel with two entrances, the one we held hands in!'

When we had been rigging the burrows earlier in the year, we had come across a burrow that ran across the slope and had two entrances. Helen and I had checked its length by reaching in to the middle from each end and were just able to touch fingers underground. We had assumed that a tunnel like this would be the last place a puffin would chose to nest, given that the wind would whistle through it and that it would be doubly vulnerable to any unwanted intruders. With that in mind, we had blocked one end with a large stone, hoping that if a bird did nest in what was now a blind burrow, we could move the stone later in the summer to introduce a camera.

It was hard to say if this was the same tunnel, but, if it was, someone or something had done away with the stone, because both ends were clear. It looked as though there had been some activity at both entrances, judging by the bare scraped earth on the threshold of each. I assumed it was the work of rabbits and leant closer for a better look. I was surprised to see an adult puffin shuffling back into the entrance that was facing west. I went to the other end and prepared the camera probe, then gently introduced it to the open entrance. I couldn't believe my eyes.

'Helen, come and look at this! There's a chick in this one,' I called.

There, on the monitor, was the fluffy backside of a puffin chick, huddled in the centre of the tunnel at a point where it took a gentle turn. The adult was still sitting in the far entrance, now looking nervous with two humans closing in on its nursery.

'I'm amazed. I didn't think they would use such an exposed nesting site. Lucky for us, eh?'

This was a hugely serendipitous find. With natural light streaming in to both ends of the nest burrow, there was no need of artificial light to reveal the goings-on within. There was also no need for elaborate pipes drilled into the walls to house a camera, since I could easily reach in from one end and position one discreetly in the ceiling of their 'pad'.

A quick forage through the tool shed at the RSPB Shetland Office by the lighthouse, and I had what I needed: a length of robust, pliable wire, some cutters and a few quickly honed wooden pegs to hold down the camera cable. I fashioned a camera mount from the wire, leaving a long spike that could be driven into the earth, and returned to the nest. I was glad to see that the adult had now gone, I hoped heading out to sea to find food for its youngster. This gave me a window in which to introduce the camera and run the cable back up the hill, secured by the wooden pegs, to a convenient hiding place behind the dry stone wall at the top of the cliff. I considered introducing a little artificial light to help reveal more of the colour below ground, but given that the chick was slate grey and muddy white and the adult, when it returned, would be the same, apart from its bill and eye of course, I decided to keep the new 'furniture' in the nest to a minimum for the time being.

I particularly wanted to record the point at which food was passed from adult to chick in the confines of the burrow. The interior of puffin nests had been filmed in the past, so I was not revealing an event that hitherto had gone unseen. That said, the footage was rare, and one cannot be certain that all puffin populations are alike in their behaviour. It had not been filmed with the birds on Shetland, as far as I was aware, and I was excited to discover if the puffin community here had peculiar traits.

Waiting for a bird to return to its nest once it has been bugged with camera equipment, however carefully hidden and unobtrusive it may be, is a tense exercise. One can hope that all will be well, but you can never be certain that the returning adult will take kindly to the changes. However tiny, any camera looks like a staring eye: the one bit you cannot camouflage is the lens. I have experimented in the past with two-way mirrors in an attempt to shroud the lens, but the reflection in these is often more disturbing for a bird than the small circle of glass in the original lens, since it can look to them as though a competitor has entered their domain. Most species are quite sanguine, but I knew from research that puffins could be surprisingly nervous when even subtle changes were made to their underground retreats.

I could empathise with their anxiety. Puffins are not the most elegant of birds in flight, their heavy bodies and narrow wings designed for 'flying' under water in pursuit of fish as much as taking to the air. They lack manoeuvrability, and landing is a hit-and-miss affair, particularly if there is little wind around to assist them with slowing down before alighting. As a result of this clumsiness, they are the frequent target of an army of pirates as they return to the nest with beaks full of food. Skuas, great and arctic, herring and black-backed gulls and even the diminutive black-headed and common gulls may all try to intercept a returning puffin and force it to give up its hard-won catch. Some of these thieves, especially great black-backed gulls and bonxies, may even attack the adult puffins directly, pulling them out of the sky and killing them as they clumsily stall and waver before landing.

For the adult puffin, therefore, the nest burrow is a sanctuary after having run the gauntlet of aerial invaders each time they return to the colony. If there is a hint that this safe retreat might be a trap, they are naturally very wary. I once witnessed an extraordinary scene on the Treshnish Isles near Mull while filming puffins nesting, when an adult otter scaled the cliffs that led to the colony. It then systematically checked each of the puffin burrows and, targeting those that were sufficiently broad to allow its invasion, squeezed inside. Five minutes later it emerged, licking its lips, and repeated the process along the cliff top until it was no more than five metres away from where I lay. I cannot be certain that the otter was eating the puffin eggs or chicks, but it seems very likely, and my presence almost certainly cut short a very thorough raid of the colony. This illustrated just how vulnerable a puffin is once it is trapped in its burrow, and goes some way towards explaining their nervousness.

Tucked out of the wind behind the wall, the image on the little screen before me showed that the chick spent a good deal of its time doing precisely nothing. From time to time it fiddled with bits of dry grass or feathers that made up the half-hearted attempt at a nest bowl on the burrow floor, but for the most part it dozed. This was a perfectly reasonable strategy for a bird whose parents could be at sea for many hours finding enough food to warrant a return to feed their chick. We were in this vigil for the long haul together. The big difference between us (apart from me being a mammal and my subject a bird) was that I had to concentrate on the image on the screen to make sure I pressed the record button if there was any action, whereas the chick could slip into blissful slumber whenever it chose. Which it did. A lot.

It was very difficult to stay focused and alert watching a pompom snoozing as first one, then two hours ticked by with no sign of an adult. I began to feel concerned that my fiddling near the nest had startled the parents sufficiently to convince them that their nest was no longer safe, but tried to temper these qualms by remembering that when I had filmed puffins returning to their colonies in the past, the gaps between hunting forays had often been very long.

After almost three hours, I noticed the chick fidgeting and shifting position a little, and, this being the highlight of the day so far, I pressed 'record' on the deck. Seconds later, the head of an adult puffin came into frame with its beak full of sand eels. It paused, staring into the camera that was now pinned to the roof of its burrow, and I held my breath. This was the moment of truth. If the adult bird was going to baulk at the changes to its nest, it would happen now.

A few seconds can feel like a very long time. But once the parent had established that the one-eyed monster staring at it from the ceiling was inanimate, it shuffled forward and delivered the fish supper to its chick. It was a gentle episode in the lives of these charming birds, repeated all over the colony hundreds of times each day, but the relief was so great from my position behind the wall that I couldn't stifle a heartfelt 'Phew!'

I continued to film the burrow throughout the rest of that and the following day, and left the camera in place so that Helen could use it to give members of the visiting public a unique insight into the puffin's private life in an upcoming open day at the reserve; part of the island's celebrations for the Shetland Nature Festival.

It is hard to keep track of the number of festivals and celebrations in Shetland each year. Some, like Up Helly Aa, have been in place for hundreds of years in one guise or another. Others, like the Flavour of Shetland, were in their infancy. The Shetland Nature Festival was a very new addition to the calendar of events. One of the driving forces behind this celebration of all things wild and wonderful was Helen Moncrieff, and at her request I had given a presentation in last year's inaugural programme. Something must have gone right (probably the fact I did it for free), and Helen had asked if I could come back again this year to chat about some of the wildlife experiences we'd had so far in Shetland. I was honoured to have been asked, and readily accepted.

The event was held in the Garrison Theatre in Lerwick, and on the night we were greeted by a full house. Ahead of me, opening the proceedings and kicking off the festivities for the coming week, would be a speech from the local MSP, Tavish Scott, and then a poetry reading from a dedicated trio from the dialect promotion group *Shetland ForWirds*. From my position backstage, sadly I was unable to hear either, but I was reliably informed that the performers had enthusiastically started their set by remarking: 'Who'd a' thought we'd be the warm-up act for Simon King?!'

# Chapter 19

## Jumplings

I would have liked to have offered more of my time to the Shetland Nature Festival, but the natural clock beyond the door of the theatre was ticking inexorably, and there were many events I had yet to film.

One that I had missed the previous year and was determined to witness this time around was the fledging of the guillemot chicks. Actually, fledging is not the correct terminology, since it infers the young birds fly from their nest as most other seabirds do. Guillemot chicks, by contrast, make a leap of faith from their cliff-top nursery long before they are able to take to the wing, and it was this remarkable and ephemeral event that I wanted to film.

Guillemots are members of the auk family, like puffins. But, unlike their cousins, they nest above ground on sea cliffs. In Shetland they come back to their breeding grounds in January but go away during high seas. In the early spring they begin to claim a tiny ledge or patch of bare rock as their nesting territory. That's it. That is the extent of home building indulged in by the species. These birds had much the same attitude to DIY as me: 'If it ain't broke, why fix it?' To be fair, laying an egg on a bare cliff ledge might seem foolhardy; after all, eggs roll don't they? Well, ordinary eggs do, but those of the guillemot are so shaped

253

that when they do wobble around they go in a tight circle, revolving around the narrow end, which is so acutely conical that it almost forms a point. Not that the single eggs are often exposed. Both parent birds take turns to incubate their annual investment, and they do so in very close proximity to their neighbours. Relations with the family next door are generally amicable, which is just as well since pairs are often nesting so close to each other that they can rub shoulders. The benefits of nesting cheek by jowl with each other are tangible when an aerial raid takes place. The sight of an approaching gull or skua causes the guillemots to forget any domestic differences and galvanises a social solidarity. As the predator flies overhead, they act as one, pointing their dagger-sharp beaks to the sky and uttering a rasping, drawn-out, wailing call. The would-be chick hunter is faced with a barrage of impenetrable spikes, beneath which the precious eggs and new-hatched chicks are guarded.

Whether it is the physical crush of this defensive society or some other force at play that has influenced the guille-mots' evolutionary strategy to get their chicks out of the nest as soon as possible is open to debate and further study, but the fact is, the young are only about twenty days old when they leave. Compare this to their close rela-tive the puffin, whose chick leaves the nest burrow when it is about fifty days old, and you begin to see that the little 'Longie Lungies', as they are known in the Shetland dialect, are pretty precocious.

Just when the guillemot chicks were going to jump was a different issue. If we had the egg-laying dates for a colony then we could have a pretty good stab at guessing when some of the chicks would leave, weather permitting. Fortunately, we had access to precisely that information, gleaned from a long-term study of the guillemots at Sumburgh Head conducted by ornithologist Martin Heubeck. His meticulous observations provided us with egg-laying dates, not just in general, but from colony to colony, which was just as well, since each collection of birds seemed to operate on its own calendar.

We had been in close touch with Helen, who is RSPB warden at Sumburgh, and it was she (once again) who tipped us off that the date was approaching when the first of the guillemot jumplings was due to go.

The astonishing run of fair weather was still with us as Marguerite and I made our way to the southern tip of the mainland. We had not rushed to the reserve in the middle of the day, knowing that the event was likely to take place at dusk, and that of course was still very late indeed due to the midsummer day length. We arrived at the breeding cliffs on a still, calm evening, and walked down the western coast to overlook one of the largest guillemot colonies on Sumburgh Head. The sun was still relatively high in the sky but its intensity was dimmed by a thickening sea mist that rolled in from the west in waves. The combination of sepia light, a natural amphitheatre populated by thousands of seabirds, and air so still that every sound from the colonies below was crystal clear: all added to the growing sense of drama and expectation about the evening ahead.

We set up our cameras and settled down for the vigil.

Now that we were in a position to study the colonies properly, we realised how tricky the task of spotting a single chick jumping to the sea below might be. If they leapt directly from their nest ledge, we would get little or no warning, and trying to spot a single, fidgety chick amongst hundreds would be a challenge. But we were banking on the father guillemots giving us a heads-up on proceedings, for it was their duty alone to lead their chick to the sea, and thereafter escort them for the early weeks of their life on the ocean wave. The adult males were likely to drop to the water ahead of their young and try to encourage them down to join them. That's what we'd been told, anyway.

Though I had filmed guillemots on many occasions previously, I had never been present when this most challenging of life events took place, and was unsure what to expect. Whilst I waited for any sign that a chick was on the move, I took the opportunity to film some of the other activity in the colony. I had a cracking view of about fifty pairs just below me and could fill the camera frame with the chicks tucked between their parents' bodies. Now and then, an adult would arrive holding a fish in its beak. Unlike puffins, guillemots only carry one fish at a time back to the nest, a hugely labour-intensive exercise, and one that is fraught with danger.

Muggers lurk in dark corners: bonxies and arctic skuas perch on crags or patrol the cliffs on the lookout for incoming birds bearing fish. Returning guillemot parents are often pursued and forced to give up their hard-won prize, further adding to the pressures of raising a family. If there are plenty of fish to be found relatively close to shore, guillemots do well, the commute to and from the feeding grounds taking less valuable time. But the further they have to travel to find a meal, the more challenging it is for guillemots to find enough to satisfy the whole family's appetite. They do have an advantage over the terns and kittiwakes, though, since they can dive to astonishing depths in search of a meal, having been recorded at a mind-boggling one-hundred and eighty metres.

The bird in front of me had dodged the pirates and was tenderly bowing its head towards its chick, nudging the fish towards its offspring's beak and stimulating it to take the meal. Both parents had their wings partly open and around the chick, shielding the youngster and the transfer of food from prying eyes overhead. The chick was a fraction of the size of its parents and covered in a black, fluffy down over its head and back, leading to white over its breast. The only hint that real feathers were on their way was a row of short quills just breaking into feather at the tip along the trailing edge of each wing and a similar emergent attempt at a tail. The little guy looked as if he needed another month to develop, but he wouldn't be getting it. Within days, perhaps even this evening, he would be making his way to the edge of the colony and throwing himself down into the sea.

The sun swept low towards the horizon in the north-west in an increasingly level angle of attack. Sea mist thickened then waned with theatrical flare across the vista before us. As it darkened, the number of patrolling skuas and gulls reduced, their day's work done, giving the guillemots their cue.

It was almost ten o'clock in the evening when Marguerite spotted an unusual movement on the cliffs halfway around the bay.

'There's one on its own. No, it's with an adult, walking down the ridge there,' she exclaimed, studying the scene through binoculars.

I trained the long lens of my camera on a razorback ridge that stuck out in a spur from part of the colony and, sure enough, there on its crest was an adult guillemot and a chick waddling close by its side, tripping and faltering on the ragged surface of rock.

'Well spotted! This is it. This little guy is going to jump any minute.' Now that we were presented with the imminent event, it seemed even more extraordinary than ever that such a tiny, seemingly ill-equipped youngster would consider jumping off a thirty-metre cliff into the sea below. Until this evening, it would not have wandered more than about thirty centimetres from the point it had hatched from the egg. It had certainly never touched the sea before. Its father looked anxious and excited, bowing his head repeatedly and shuffling ever closer to a point on the cliff ledge where he could go no further. The chick too bobbed up and down with such vigour that it looked in danger of losing its balance and toppling off the precipice.

With no warning besides a particularly deep head bow, the adult bird launched from the crag and fluttered down to the sea below, leaving the chick stranded, alone and with little choice but to follow. It was clear now why they had waited for dusk, when the number of predatory birds had reduced. The chick was incredibly vulnerable, and would have made an easy meal for any passing skua or gull.

'It's going to go. This is it!' I said, watching the jumpling bobbing even more excitedly than before; and then it was away, launching from the rock with a mighty leap – well, as mighty a leap as its stubby legs could manage. It plummeted almost vertically down towards the sea, little wing-stalks spread and fluttering, disproportionately large webbed feet spread out behind; all helping to provide as broad a surface area as possible to slow the descent, which, nonetheless, looked terrifyingly fast. The chick hit the water, popped up like a cork and was immediately joined by its father, which swam close by its side, steering it towards the open sea.

'That was amazing! Soooooo sweet.' Marguerite was scanning the cliffs for any more adventurous youngsters preparing to take the plunge. 'Here comes another.'

Scrabbling along precisely the same section of cliff, we saw a lone adult displaying all the behavioural traits of the one before, head bowing and anxiously shuffling towards the edge. But there was no sign of a chick. I thought at first it must be a reluctant traveller, hanging back in the colony, until I noticed a movement on the sheer rock face below the father.

'There it is. It must have slipped. Oh dear, that doesn't look too good.'

The chick was some three or four metres down the rock face below its father and desperately trying to join him. With little wings spread akimbo she used her big webbed feet to clamber up the near vertical slope towards her father. For every step she managed to make, she slipped back again half the distance. The father looked beside himself with concern, bowing, dipping and shuffling to and fro on the ledge, looking down at his youngster. The chick got to within a few centimetres of the top when she lost her footing completely. She tumbled head over heels and, in an uncontrolled spin, hurtled towards the sea. Her father immediately followed, flying fast to the bay below, but there was nothing he could do to ease his offspring's plight. The chick hit the water first, with a substantial splash for one so tiny, and disappeared beneath the surface. The father was on the spot in an instant, in time to see his chick pop back up, totally saturated but otherwise, apparently, none the worse for her ordeal.

Marguerite and I whooped with relief and joy. This was turning into one of the most riveting natural dramas we had seen played out on the isles so far. It was not simply the 'heart-in-mouth' action that was so compelling, but also the epic story that surrounded the chicks now that they were in the water for the first time in their lives. Their journey had only just begun. As the sodden little chick paddled hard alongside her dad, she was starting an unbroken life on the ocean wave that would span at least the next month, perhaps longer, before she would be able to fly properly for the first time. In that period she would continue paddling, diving and honing her swimming skills, all the time being fed and cared for her dad.

But for me the most extraordinary detail in the story of the lives of these little birds – once they had made the leap of faith from the cliffs – was that they would now paddle a course all the way to the coast of Norway. Almost all of the guillemots that breed in Shetland make this epic journey, over several weeks of hard paddling. It may be that traditional rich fishing grounds there are incentive enough to drive the parent birds to encourage their chicks to paddle the two hundred miles or so over the open ocean. There may be other factors at play, but the truth is, no one knows.

We took some time with our own little chick the following day, around the house we were renting on farmland on the east mainland. Shetland is not just a mecca for birdlife: for the flowering plants that can withstand the fickle weather, there is nowhere better.

Many of the fields are 'unimproved'. Never has there been a more inappropriate word created by man in relation to grassland. An 'improved' field has very likely been ploughed, covered with herbicide, insecticide and fertilizer, planted with a fast-growing, nutrient-packing grass variety and cut for animal feed at least twice a year. Maybe a cow or two will be allowed to wander on it from time to time, but otherwise it will be void of virtually all other life.

An 'unimproved' pasture will have nothing but livestock and perhaps a bit of muck put on it from time to time. It will not be drained and so will have soggy corners that harbour rushes and other wetland species and, because of the lack of chemicals, it will be home to myriad broad-leafed herbs, or weeds as we may call them, and the invertebrate life that comes with them.

Improved pasture is effectively a natural desert: give me unimproved grasslands any day. And, for that matter, give my kids the same, please. All my children – my older three from my first marriage, Alexander, Romy and Greer, and now Savannah – have known the joy of running barefoot through fields that vibrate with the colour of wild flowers. In the fields around our little house in Shetland were quite literally carpets of daisies. I had rarely seen so many spread over such wide areas. Some fields had the look of a covering of snow at a distance, so dense were the nodding white heads.

Savannah spent hours hunched over the dancing yellow and white faces, picking great handfuls and bringing them to us as gifts. Before long, we had a collection of jam jars, mugs and plastic food tubs stuffed with bunches of daisies all around the house.

I suppose I should say that all wild flowers should be left to grow where they sprout for others to enjoy, to do the job for which they were intended in furthering the next generation of plants, and to nourish the legions of insects that depend on them. I should say that, but I won't. There are laws, of course, that prohibit the picking of wild flowers on nature reserves and on private land without the owner's permission. And, sadly, there are some species that are now so rare and vulnerable that they need all the help they can get simply to survive. All this is perfectly right and reasonable. But to tell a child who is lost in the wonder of collecting huge handfuls of nature's jewels that she must stop will serve only to alienate her from the world around her. It is through collecting flowers, catching beetles, chasing butterflies and examining a crab in the hand that we may find a route to being a part of the natural world. Only when one cares about a tiny natural detail does one notice its passing, and I hope that letting Savannah, and my other children, run feral from time to time through fields of flowers, and picking a few (common ones) along the way will encourage them to fight to ensure such marvels survive for the wonder and edification of their own children.

Blimey, all that spawned from a few daisies.

A call from naturalist Brydon Thomason soon after our guillemot filming adventure shifted our focus sharply away from the cliffs and on to the open sea. He had been liaising with the killer whale scientists on a boat in northern waters, and had encountered a large number of orcas hunting herring there. The moment he got back to land he informed us of the marvellous spectacle he had witnessed, and we moved quickly, dropping plans we had in place in order to accommodate the promise of more contact with these dynamic sea wolves.

We were to meet the scientists, Brydon and the crew of the *Julie Rose*, a fast, modern boat that takes folk on day trips around the North Isles, in Cullivoe Harbour on the north of Yell. Another blinder of a day greeted us and warmed the ferry crossing, promising calm seas for our venture into the north Atlantic. After a speedy but legal drive up the length of Yell, we met Andy Foote of the University of Aberdeen, Volker Deecke and members of the NAKID project (standing for 'North Atlantic Killer

Whale IDentification') on the quayside to discuss a strategy for the day ahead. The team was still buzzing with excitement from the previous day's observations, and Volker, who was working with the University of St Andrews, had made some extraordinary underwater sound recordings of the action. To gather his data he had combined science with cooking: not following the Heston Blumenthal school of cuisine, but with an ingenious adaptation of cookware. As I studied the parabolic reflector he was using to concentrate sound under the water to a single focal point where a hydrophone was mounted, I realised I was in fact looking at a wok, covered with a neoprene skin! It proved to be perfect for listening out for orcas and other cetaceans, and was robust enough to take the punishing marine environment. If all else failed, Volker could always knock up a quick chicken chow mein.

Whilst we waited for our boat to join us from its mooring on Unst, we listened to some of the recordings made by Volker from the day before. The first included some very loud squeaks and whistles that Volker felt might be signature calls. Killer whales are in fact not whales at all, but the largest members of the dolphin family of cetaceans. All the evidence available suggests they are extremely bright and have complex and enduring relationships within an extended family and with neighbouring groups of orcas. These sounds could well have been individuals in a group calling each other by name. There is a lot of evidence to suggest signature calls are common amongst many species of dolphin and could be used to coordinate hunting strategies, sort out domestic issues, or, perhaps, simply to engage in cetacean conversation. When you consider that orcas and other dolphins can 'see' the world about them with sound, using sonar to build up a picture of their physical environment, then it is conceivable that they can communicate these 'images' to each other with copies of the same sound. It's a bit like someone transmitting a TV picture straight into your eyes. Pretty handy if you want to pass on information about a shoal of fish you've detected, or perhaps the topography of a stretch of coastline, and all the better if you can direct your message to a chosen individual. A hypothetical orca conversation might go something like this:

'Hey George.'

'Yes, Griselda.'

'Take a look a this: squeak, tic-tic-tic, rattle, rattle, ping!'

'Wow, niiiiice!'

You get the picture, or they do, or something.

The next recording was taken in the heat of the orca-hunting activity on a large herring shoal. Again, there were many clicks and whistles being uttered by a number of different killers, but one sound stood out from the static of their conversation: a piercing whistle, rising at the end, followed quickly by a dull crack. Volker believed this was the point at which an orca had closed in on the fish shoal and made a kill. The loud sweeping whistle might well be desperately uncomfortable for the fish, causing them to shoal tighter in a fright response, and the cracking sound was made as the great tail fluke of the orca was used to smash into the shoal, stunning fish that could then be sucked up with ease. It was tantalising stuff and gave me a boost of optimism that we might be on to something very special today.

Amongst the many boxes of toys, also known as equipment, that I had with me, was included a pole-cam. This is the affectionate term given to a camera in an underwater housing on a stick. If we were lucky enough to encounter hunting orcas, I might be able to reveal their activity beneath the surface, and that was an exciting prospect.

The *Julie Rose* arrived as the killer whale team prepared to leave harbour in their RIB. With two different high-speed vessels searching the open sea, keeping in touch by marine band radio, we stood a better chance of encountering the orcas than sticking together. The researchers would be stopping from time to time to 'listen' for activity using the wok-cum-hydrophone, and we would be able to cruise in another area where herring had recently been seen by the local fishing fleet, scanning the horizon for visual clues that orcas might be feeding. Our journey out to the north took us past Hermaness, where we had walked with Savannah in the rain a few weeks before, then Muckle Flugga, a barren island bearing the most northerly lighthouse in Britain, and Out Stack, a bare rock that represented the last shred of terrestrial Britain before the open sea. Leaving Shetland behind, we continued on a northerly heading before striking out to the west where Brydon had seen the orcas the day before.

I have had the good fortune to travel over many of the world's seas in search of great wildlife events. In the Antarctic Ocean I scoured the horizon for flocks of birds that might betray the presence of krill shoals, sailing in gargantuan seas that rose and fell fifteen metres. I filmed flocks of tiny seabirds called prions, battling against the gales, and wandering albatross following alongside our ship with immense wing tips almost touching my camera lens. In the waters around the Azores I had followed dolphins and flocks of Cory's shearwaters, looking for bait balls that would attract whales and sharks, and in South Africa I had filmed – from the air – vast shoals of sardines as they were corralled by staggering congregations of dolphins, with whales bursting through the centre of the maelstrom. I wondered how this journey into the seas around a place I had come to love so dearly would, or could, compare with these world-class spectacles.

We cruised at a fair pace for over half an hour, the land slipping away into the blue haze of the distant horizon, when I saw in the north a tiny flicker of white against the blue sky. Studying the point through binoculars, I could see that gannets and other seabirds were working in circles over what must have been a fish shoal, and a ripple of excitement ran down my spine.

'Birds ahead,' I yelled. That was before I had had time to study the scene properly. With binoculars still to my eyes, I panned left and right to see where the flock ended and started to think that perhaps I had made a mistake. There was no end to the flock. It looked like the entire horizon was carpeted with the far-off forms of seabirds circling and shifting in search of food. Surely this was an optical illusion created by the unusually warm air and distance creating a light-play that looked like birds? But no, as I studied harder, there could be no doubt. Hundreds upon hundreds of aerial hunters were swooping over the sea about two miles ahead of us. The skipper opened up the throttle and added to the adrenalin rush by powering his craft towards the scene. The huge flock of birds working an area of ocean on this scale was a sure sign of fish, lots of fish. Where there were fish there could be other hunters in the sea, hunters like killer whales. The closer we got to the flocks, the bigger they seemed to get. We were entering another world, the true dominion of the gannet, the guillemot, the puffin and the gull. When we watched and filmed these birds on their nesting cliffs, we were seeing a creature that was metaphorically pinioned, forced to tame down its wild, wandering spirit to raise a family. But here, on the open sea, they were free, dynamic and in control. This air belonged to them, and here they twisted and tumbled with grace and ease, unseen to all but the most fortunate human eye. Within minutes we were among them and then, quite suddenly, a yell from Brydon.

'Dolphins. There Simon, off the port side.' I ran to the rail and looked across the flat water. A sudden flurry of scythe-shaped fins cut through the surface some fifty metres away.

'White-sided, I think,' Brydon added, his voice tight with excitement. 'Yes there, definitely. Oh wow, loads of 'em!'

A group of ten, maybe fifteen dolphins were belting along beside us, but as I allowed my gaze to cast over a wider stretch of water, I realised they were everywhere.

Wherever I looked, the water was being cut into white plumes by the surfacing backs of dolphins. I had no idea how many: perhaps a hundred, maybe two hundred animals, zig-zagging below the hundreds of plunging gannets. It was a scene of mass ocean feeding to rival any I had witnessed elsewhere in the world, but it was here, in British waters, in Shetland.

'Fabulous Brydon, really awesome,' I called back.

It felt as though the full force of the feeding storm had subsided, though: hundreds of birds were loafing on the surface of the sea, clearly sated, and though some flocks were still playing leapfrog on fish shoals into the distance, the energy of the activity was waning. We all searched hard for a hint of a great black fin that would betray the presence of an orca, but it was not to be. They were not here or, at least, not now. Such is the dynamic nature of life and death on the open sea. A radio call to the scientists established that they had not been lucky with the search for killer whales either and, after filming the birds and dolphins for a while, we decided to extend our search further still.

A couple of hours' fruitless vigil and we had to reluctantly turn back towards land. We continued to study the waves, but the chances of a sighting and the sense of optimism that we might encounter orcas slipped away as the mass of Hermaness loomed ever greater in our path. Before we reached land, I was able to reflect on what we had just witnessed.

Most of us are inevitably preoccupied by life on land. It's perfectly reasonable for terrestrial mammals like us to be so. Never mind that the vast majority of our planet is covered by sea, and that every day and night, all over the world's oceans, there are natural events playing out on an unimaginable scale. It doesn't really affect us, right? Wrong.

What we had just seen might have been a thrilling highlight for us, but for the denizens of the ocean it was commonplace. It made me feel at once edified and optimistic, and at the same time vulnerable and helpless. We have caused untold damage to life in the oceans in the past; we do so still. For all the same reasons that the big blue remains an enigma to most, the sea is a conveniently unwatched and under-policed resource that has been repeatedly raped without penalty. The fabulous display of life we had just witnessed was cause for hope, but it was also reason to be mindful that a huge web of life forms depend on the seas and that while our indiscriminate abuse of them might go unnoticed in the short term, in the long term we would all be impoverished as a consequence.

# Chapter 20

## Night Fairies

We had passed the summer solstice by a week or so and already the light in the night sky was dimming. Everything about the climate and the seasons in Shetland is capricious, from the wind to the rapid shift from summer towards autumn. We still had weeks of long days ahead of us, but the year had made the turn and I, along with the wild inhabitants of the isles, had a sense of urgency to get as much done and seen as possible in the time left to us.

For over a year now, we had hoped to go on a camping trip with Savannah to one of the islands on the east coast to witness a very special natural event. Mousa, south of Lerwick, is managed as a nature reserve by the RSPB, and hosts a wonderful variety of breeding birds, from arctic skuas and red-throated divers to black guillemots and large tern colonies. It is also the nesting place for almost ten per cent of the British population of storm petrels, diminutive seabirds that lead an enigmatic lifestyle, only coming in to land in the dead of night. It was these, above all, we wanted to see.

Mousa was famous, not just for its wildlife, but for one of the best-preserved prehistoric buildings in Europe, too, a two thousand-year-old stone-built tower called a broch, in an astonishingly good state of repair. Brochs are found all over Scotland – there are well over five hundred of them in all – and about one hundred of those are in Shetland, but the Mousa broch stands tall amongst them: thirteen metres high, to be precise. Just what purpose it served to the folk who built it in 100 BC (or thereabouts) is the subject of some debate. It is often referred to as a fort, and it may well have been used as a sanctuary in times of siege but, for a number of reasons, not least of which is the lack of any strategically placed arrow slits from which warriors within could fire out at their enemies, its defensive role is questionable. Brochs were undoubtedly lived in, and might well have been status symbols for their owners, but whatever their original purpose, they were built to last. Ingenious double-skinned walls made with thousands of tons of rock with no mortar rise up to form what looks like a small version of a power station cooling tower. All vestiges of the timber flooring and buildings within the Mousa broch have long since disappeared, but the tower remains an imposing feature on the western shore of the island.

It was the contemporary occupants of the broch that we wanted to see now, since many of the storm petrels that nested on the island found sanctuary in gaps between stones in the building's wall. Pete Ellis calls it 'Britain's Biggest Bird Box'. To stand a chance of witnessing their return to their nest sites would require an all-night vigil, and we prepared our camping gear and sufficient provisions for a couple of days' living before driving to the little port near Sandwick on the mainland.

# Night Fairies

We planned to meet the *Solan IV*, the ferry owned by Tom Jamieson who had helped us with the gannet filming, on a morning when the unbroken warmth and calm of summer had decided to take a rest. The wind had lifted considerably, and a large swell brought rolling waves crashing against the pier at Sandsayre where Tom was to pick us up. There was the threat of drizzle in the air, too – just our luck for the one time we intended to camp with our daughter; but in fact these conditions all worked in our favour in terms of our mission to see the petrels. The reason the sparrow-sized seabirds only come to the land under the cover of darkness is their terrible vulnerability. On the wing they are nimble and swift, a challenge for any skua or gull to catch and kill over the waves. But the evolutionary sacrifice made for being so beautifully adapted for a life on the open sea is a desperate clumsiness on land. Their long legs and webbed feet are perfect for dancing off the tops of the mightiest waves, dipping down to pick up minute planktonic food particles, but on land the legs are set so far back on the body that the best the birds can manage is an ungainly waddle. If they were spotted in this vulnerable position by any avian predator they would be killed in moments, so they use the cloak of darkness to shroud their terrestrial visits. Even a clear moonlit night can make them less confident about coming ashore, and so the cloud, the wind and, within reason, the rain all worked in their, and our, favour.

'Morning Tom, how are you?' I called across from the slipway to the cabin as he masterfully brought his craft alongside.

'Fine Simon, fine . . . Swelly old day, eh? Don't worry, it's a lovely day at Mousa.'

I laughed, thinking at first that Tom was being sarcastic. The island was less than a mile from the mainland across Mousa Sound. How different could it be? But Tom assured me he wasn't joking as we set off into the pitch and roll of the swell.

Savannah thought that the crossing was great fun, enjoying the sensation of her stomach lifting on the roller-coaster dips made by the boat and giggling as the ship's bell rang in celebration of each dramatic shudder caused by an oncoming wave. I was less amused. If this weather persisted, then camping was going to be a challenge with a two and a half year old.

I should never have doubted Tom, of course. As we steamed into the waters protected by the north end of the island, it was like entering another world: the sea levelled out, the wind dropped and, by the time we reached the jetty at West Ham, there was a hint of sunshine behind the high cloud.

Marguerite, Savannah and I were being joined by Alison Pinkney, our wonderful production team-mate who had been filming events when Marguerite and I were not working alone. It's worth mentioning at this late stage that many of our adventures were shadowed, in the nicest possible sense, by Alison, or, before her, Nick Jordan. The TV series we were making included elements of our life on the island as well as the wildlife, and it was crucial that someone was able to record the adventures we all shared. Marguerite could and did film Savannah and me, but someone had to film us as a family whenever possible. The great talent of these people was to be unobtrusive and passive observers, occasionally asking us questions that might prompt a response that would clarify a situation. But we were careful to ensure that our experiences on Shetland were honest and personal and, to this end, Alison was to camp away from our pitch on Mousa and behave as a 'fly on the wall'.

We hauled all our equipment up the jetty to the little stone hut used by the Sinclairs, who keep sheep on the island, and the RSPB as a store for maintenance equipment and very occasional lodging. We had been given permission to use the hut as a place to put any gear that was not immediately essential, and Alison earmarked it as her sanctuary for the night. Savannah noticed immediately that it was a little untidy, a good layer of dust covered almost everything and the corners were thick with cobwebs.

'Your house is messy!' she said as pointedly and innocently as only a young child can. Alison was quick to point out that this was not her house, she was just borrowing it for the night, and that her own house was really quite tidy, thank you.

Savannah took this on board and continued helping to pull the last of the bags into the store, when something caught her eye.

It is uncanny how well tuned and developed the search image for toys is in a two and a half year old. Where I had been muddling about with camera kit, and only seen brooms, shovels and Tilley lamps in the store, she homed in on a white bucket that contained something colourful and plastic. Supermarket managers are well aware of this uncanny ability in small children, and plant shiny things and sweets at their level around the store, which miraculously find their way into the shopping trolley, only to be discovered by parents at the check-out where many are then too embarrassed to send them back from whence they came for fear of being branded cruel and hard-nosed.

Savannah arrived in the doorway of the stone hut sporting a mask with the face of a cow.

Now, correct me if I'm being dim, but I can't think of any reason why a cow mask might help with the study of nesting birds. Even the most optimistic researcher would not pass as a bovid simply by sporting it, so it couldn't be a disguise to enable a close approach to timid creatures. When I later asked about the collection of masks, plastic swords and other fancy-dress kit hiding in the corner of the store, I was informed it was for a time-line activity for school parties visiting the island on educational visits. Yeah, right. I have a suspicion they were there to offer research scientists a bit of light relief after long days of gathering data in the field. What better way to unwind than to sit back with a nice cup of tea, wearing a cow mask? Maybe not, then.

Whilst Savannah happily trotted around the beach mooing, Marguerite and I made ready for the short hike over the island to the broch. We struck out on the journey laden with gear, with Savannah, now back to her normal pretty-faced self, perched on my shoulders. As we crested the hill and saw the broch clearly for the first time, I asked her who she thought might live in the tower of stone.

'Princesses!' she said gleefully.

We pitched the tent in a protected paddock away from the broch, with plenty of time still to spare before nightfall. Though Savannah had spent a good part of her tender years already under canvas, it had all been in Kenya, in tents where a normal double bed and a shower were available. This was the first time she had been camping proper, and she, and we, loved it. I know it can be miserable if the weather turns sour and you get wet and cold with nowhere to dry off. But there is something about pitching your home where you stop your travels for the day that I believe appeals to a deep-rooted part of our ancestral selves. Our distant, primitive ancestors quite probably roamed the plains of Africa by day in search of food. But as dusk fell, they would probably have sought sanctuary on cliffs or trees to avoid the attention of night-prowling predators. The instinct to 'pitch camp' as a close-knit family unit would have been overwhelming, and perhaps a vestige of that need remains in us to this day, explaining the simple pleasure gleaned from setting up a temporary home with your family.

With camp and camera kit now organised, we decided to explore the island a little before nightfall, walking over the South Isle towards the open sea. En route, we passed a small freshwater loch and paused to watch and film arctic skuas that had arrived here to bathe and drink. Savannah got to grips with operating the camera and long lens to film the birds, but decided that when I took the helm she had a better plan. As I prepared to run the tape on the skua that was indulging in a particularly vigorous

spot of bathing, the image went a hazy pink then disappeared altogether. I took my eye away from the eyepiece
to find Savannah with her face pressed against the lens,
giggling and saying, 'Look at me, Daddy!'

Taking the hint, we walked on to the lagoon on the
southeast coast, where common seals regularly hauled out,
many with their newborn pups. Their nursery area is
restricted from public access for good reason, the seals
can be very jumpy when they have young, so after a distant
view we decided to head back to the tent and prepare for
the evening.

By now Savannah was starting to flag and it was clear
she wouldn't last until the petrels arrived after dark. The
cloud had thickened once more, though, cutting the light
from the late evening sky, and there was a chance this
gloaming would stimulate the birds sitting on their nests
to start calling, giving Savannah the chance to witness
their unearthly song first hand. As we neared the broch,
her little grip on my hand grew firmer. The structure
cut an imposing, dark figure against the slate-grey sky
and I could sense her imagination building dragons and
unknown beasts within its walls. I comforted her by
saying there was nothing nasty here, just night fairies,
and if we were lucky we would hear them talking to
each other.

She clutched me tighter as we pushed open the iron gate
to the small doorway that led to the broch's interior, step-
ping into a profound darkness. The thick walls had brought
night prematurely inside the building, and I switched on
my head torch to better see where I was going. Savannah's

eyes were saucer wide, her little moon face staring up at the circle of brighter sky above the main chamber.

'Let's listen for the fairies for a bit, Babba,' I whispered. 'They are little birds really, called petrels, but we can call them fairies. Some of them are sleeping in these walls right now, sitting on their eggs, but they'll soon be waking up and then they'll start to sing.'

For a few minutes we stood in near perfect silence. All wind was excluded by the thick walls, and I could hear only the gentle whistling of Savannah's breathing. Then the first chuckling call came from the far side of the main chamber. A reedy, nasal 'errr-CHIP' started the proceedings that then began to wind into a mechanical, whirring churr, regularly interrupted with a high hiccup as the bird took a breath. Once under way, the song can continue for many minutes on end and, as one bird starts, so another picks up the tune and delivers its own rendition from deep inside its nest chamber. The main purpose of the call seems to be to advertise that a nest is occupied, and it may also help the returning mate to home in on its breeding chamber, though pairs stay together for life, and return each year to nest in the same cavity, so they must become quite used to where their 'home' is.

All around us the walls began to hum and whirr with the calls of the petrels, and a broad grin spread over Savannah's face.

'Night fairies, Daddy, they're talking!' she whispered, then added, 'Sleepy time now.'

I carried her back to the tent a little way up the hill and she was asleep in my arms by the time I reached it.

I tucked her into her sleeping bag and returned to film the arrival of the petrels from the sea. Each of the parent birds takes its turn to incubate the single egg, usually sitting for about three days before their partner returns from feeding at sea to swap shifts.

A boat party of visitors had just arrived, brought by Tom on his scheduled midnight visit to Mousa, which allows people to experience the marvel of the petrels first hand. We kept back, not wanting to clutter their experience with all our camera kit, and, if I'm honest, not wanting to break the magic of having the island to ourselves. By the time the last of the visitors had left an hour or so later, the activity around the broch was in full swing. Looking up the outside walls against the faint grey light of the sky, I could see the tiny moth-like forms fluttering around the ramparts. Within the building, the chorus of voices was in full swing, and I could see several flying against the dim circle of sky above the main chamber. We were careful with every footstep, knowing that the petrels were very clumsy on the ground and that there may be one or two scrabbling around in search of their mate. We were glad of our caution when we encountered a bird on the floor of the passageway just inside the door, and were able to step over it carefully to get into the main chamber.

Using a mini camera on a stick, I looked into one or two of the nest tunnels and managed to find an incubating bird that, though a little perplexed, allowed me to film it sitting on its egg.

Outside again, we found a newly arrived bird with its head in a tiny cavity in the wall, but the rest of its body fully exposed, wings fluttering, long legs scrabbling as it attempted to squeeze inside. It stayed in this position for a minute or more and reminded us just how vulnerable these birds would be to predators if they attempted this sort of manoeuvre in broad daylight.

A hint of first light crept into the sky in the northeast, and with it the sounds and sights of the storm petrels abruptly dropped away.

By dawn, we were all tucked up in the tent for a snooze before making breakfast and heading back to meet Tom by midday. Tents packed away, we regrouped with Alison on the jetty, who had managed to snatch a couple of hours' sleep after filming through the night, and Marguerite asked her how she had enjoyed her supper. We had come with basic supplies, including a staple of a certain brand of dried noodle meals, to which one only had to add water.

Alison held Marguerite's eye for a moment before responding with deadpan irony. 'Deeeeelicious!'

# Chapter 21

## *Just a Beginning*

When filming wildlife, one must always be able to adapt. So although I was getting ready to try and film arctic skuas chasing terns in flight, a phone call from Helen soon changed my priorities.

'Orcas Simon. They've been seen near Sumburgh. At least five, we think. I'm heading there now for a look.'

'Helen, thank you. We're on our way,' I answered, already pushing camera cases back into the Land Rover and checking the map to identify the headland Helen had mentioned.

We had not seen any killer whales since last year, and the chance of an encounter was reason enough to drop everything and try and catch up with them. It was especially so because we did not have long before we had to leave Shetland for projects in the south. This could be our one and only chance to see them this year.

After a drive of twenty minutes or so, we had a call from Helen saying she had lost them, and there was no telling where they had gone. They were last seen heading up the west coast and we were faced with the prospect of another disappointing near miss. We slowed our pace and started to pull the car into every lay-by that had a view of the sea to scan the water for a sign of a fin.

Nothing. Killer whales may be big, but the sea looks a lot bigger when they are not in it. After half an hour searching I began to consider cutting our losses and getting back to the skuas and terns when I got another excited call from Helen.

'They've been seen again, Simon, heading up the east coast now.' These orcas had a sense of humour. We had been searching the wrong coastline completely. We drove back to the highest point we could find on a tiny loop road near Dalsetter, and once again scoured the sea with binoculars.

'Got 'em!' I yelled to Marguerite. 'They're a long way off, but they're definitely orcas. It looks like they've got something.'

With the magnification of my telephoto lens improving the view by more than thirty times, I could see at least four orcas splashing and spy hopping offshore about a mile away. The fact that they were staying in one spot and making such a kerfuffle suggested they already had prey, and later careful analysis of the footage showed that they were indeed batting a seal about in the water and eating it.

We were soon joined by Helen, her mum and a number of other people who had heard the news on the orca grapevine. At one point a young killer leapt almost entirely clear of the water, creating a massive splash on his return, and though it was an awfully long way off, the display brought a loud squeal of delight from everyone gathered. Such is the charisma of these wonderful creatures, and their ability to draw you into their world. The closest analogy I can find in the human world would be the effect on the crowd of a mega pop star, let's say Elvis, playing a concert in Wembley Stadium. If you happened to be sitting near the back of the audience, the best you could hope to see of your idol would be a distant speck, brightly lit on the stage. But you would live every move, share every perceived nuance and cheer at every gyration, despite the distance. Orcas have that presence. You may see only a splash, a speck of black dorsal fin, a tiny flash of a white belly, but your mind's eye carries you close by their side, takes you into the depths with their slick black bodies and you live their movements as if they were alongside you.

The pod of killers appeared to finish their meal and seemed to be heading north. A thought dawned on us. They were moving in the direction of Mousa Sound. If we could get there before them and, better still, get on a boat, then we stood the very slim chance of seeing them in closer proximity.

I once again called on the amiable Tom Jamieson to see if he had time to take us out on the *Solan IV*, and he readily agreed, as excited – it seemed – at the prospect of a close encounter with the orcas as we all were. We had heard from the research team, too, who had reacted to the report by scrambling their RIB; they were soon to be on the water, hoping to catch up with the killers.

We found ourselves back in precisely the same spot in which we'd first received the call from Helen notifying us about the orcas. Together with Helen, and her friend Harriet who had worked on the killer whale project the previous year, we quickly loaded all the camera gear on to the boat and cast off.

I was careful not to invest too high an expectation in

the venture. The orcas had proved, both in the far north and today, that their movements could be very unpredictable and fast. If they chose to head out to the open sea, which they might well now they had eaten, we would not catch up with them. If they decided to turn around and head back around Sumburgh Head, we would not see them. We were hoping for a tiny possibility to come good – that they would decide to swim directly towards Mousa Sound – and I was pragmatic about the chances of that happening.

Tom held a steady course south, and after ten minutes Harriet made mobile phone contact with the research team who had managed to locate the pod and were with them. I envied their streamlined operation, but was hugely grateful too that we had been given a chance of seeing the killers. A tense five minutes passed as we scanned the calm blue water for any sign of them, before I noticed the research RIB in the distance off the port side.

'They must be close,' I called to Tom, 'Andy and the crew are up ahead. Oh, there's one now!'

I had glimpsed a fin almost dead ahead, about five hundred metres away. I couldn't contain my excitement now. The orcas were near and we were bang in line with their path. Tom steered the *Solan* towards the sighting before killing the engines and allowing her to drift.

The sudden quiet and stillness added a further frisson of expectation to the mood. I had flashes of the scene in the movie *Jaws*, as the crew of the ill-fated and ironically named boat, the *Orca*, wait for a sign that the deadly giant shark is approaching.

'Look, look, look!' A squeal of delight from Helen brought my gaze away from the starboard side and back to port where the great fin of a bull orca rose much closer than before.

'Here they come; they're coming right alongside,' I said as I prepared to film at a point in the water where I had seen the cryptic shadows of at least two great forms beneath the surface. And then they were with us.

Until this moment, everyone had been whooping and cheering with every glimpse of the killers as they approached, but now, with two adults no more than five metres away, the whole boat fell silent. We could see their backs through the clear green-blue water, passing almost beneath the hull, the white eye-patches twisting organically through the refracted surface. The vision was dreamlike and suspended in time until first one, then the second broke the surface to take a breath. In this brief act, lasting no more than a few seconds, I felt a clear and profound empathy with the orcas. For just a moment we shared the same space, our bodies were no more than a few metres apart; we gulped the same air. The spirits of the deep had graced us with their presence, and for each of us on board the *Solan IV* that day, the precise detail of the encounter will remain forever clear and very personal.

As the pair rolled and sank beneath the surface, I found that I was holding my breath, not willing to allow the slightest sound to sully the perfect, powerful tranquillity.

But it was not over. Another group of females and young calves cruised close by the boat, then still more. Soon we didn't know which way to look; there seemed to be killer whales everywhere: some of them in the mid-distance; others close enough that we could hear them, and, if they were upwind, smell their breath.

'How many have you seen?' I asked Marguerite in a hushed tone.

'I'm not sure. Fifteen maybe? Perhaps more. Here comes another one!' She pointed out the fin of another great bull that was catching up with the rest of the party.

The experience had taken me beyond an adrenalin rush and into a zone of pure joy. With later close scrutiny of the film, and in conversation with the scientists, we were able to identify at least twenty individual orcas, a staggering number this close to shore and a record for the NAKID study from inshore waters. Volker had recorded the sounds they were making and revealed that the conversation had been near constant and very excited. Cross-references with previous records showed that this was at least two family groups coming together, and included several individuals new to the project. We had struck orca gold. For a while, the orcas allowed us to follow alongside at a distance as they cruised towards the mainland, turning south again and heading back in the direction of Sumburgh. Then they decided to shift up a gear, and the next time we saw them surface they had travelled a good two hundred metres ahead of the boat. I went in to the cabin to talk to Tom.

'Thank you so much, that was simply marvellous,' I said, shaking his hand. 'Let's not try to keep up – time to let them go, I think. They've already done us proud.'

They had made their intentions clear, and the least we

could do was respect that by allowing them their space.

Once back on shore, we piled the camera gear back into the car and headed south in the hope that we might catch another glimpse of the orcas from land. We were not disappointed. By the time we reached Grutness near Sumburgh, an adult bull was hunting close to shore, and we watched as he cruised to within a few metres of where we had spotted a rather panicked-looking common seal moments before. The orca cruised back out to open water and we saw the seal resurface, with a 'Phew!' written all over its face.

A fast, breathless run with the camera up the east cliffs of Sumburgh caught another group of three or four, hugging the rocks in classic seal-searching mode before they disappeared around the head, and a dash across to the west coast caught two of them swimming across the voe towards the Ness of Burgi, almost literally into the sunset.

The evening sun cast a warm sepia light across the sea where their ripples still lingered and on to the scene before me. A group of ten or fifteen people had gathered on the cliff top to watch the killer whales and now, the natural show over, they turned to each other in conversation. Before me was a microcosm of all that had attracted me to Shetland in the beginning, and what would always compel me to return. A harmonious blend of natural splendour, unpredictable wildlife, of light and distance, of a community who knew they were part of something very special and were grateful for it without pretension. And, for a moment, I felt a part of it too.

# Epilogue

You cannot start a love affair and then simply walk away from it. Well, I can't anyway. The months we spent in Shetland between the spring of 2008 and the late summer of 2009 were of course part of a television project, but that was not why we were there. We were in Shetland because first I, and then my family, had grown to love it. We have entered a new phase in our relationship with the islands in the north; a more mature chapter that has new richness and depth. We have many good friends in the islands now who are important in our lives, some of whom have featured in these pages, some of whom played little or no part in our search for wildlife but who extended us true hospitality, care and ready smiles.

We returned to Shetland in the September of 2009, though not to film. The schedule for the series was over. We returned on our own terms, to catch up with friends, and to immerse ourselves in the magic of the isles without some of the inevitable pressures that occur when you are living and working at the same time. We almost immediately stumbled into another festival, this time featuring guitar maestros from around the world. Savannah played with her friends from the house next door, and Marguerite and I went in search of otters, to photograph them but also just to watch them. We spent a magical day following a dog otter in the territory by the lagoon, sitting in the rocks no more than ten metres away as he slept in the seaweed exposed by the dropping tide.

Where once I visited Shetland, now I go back there.

The islands found their way into my bloodstream by reputation and now they are in my very bones through rich experience. They will remain unpredictable, capricious, beautiful and sometimes hostile. But Shetland will, I hope, always harbour a wealth of natural wonders that with time, consideration, sensitivity and care will offer themselves to a patient lover.

# Picture Acknowledgements

Charlie Hamilton James: 3 bottom, 25 bottom. Ivan Hawick: 8 top, 10 top, 11 top and bottom, 16 top, 29 bottom, 32. Martin Hughes-Games: 5 top. Simon King: 2 top, 4 top, 9, 12 bottom, 14 top, 15 top and bottom, 16 bottom, 17 bottom, 30 top, 31 top and bottom. Jamie McPherson: 1, 18 top, 19 top. Marguerite Smits van Oyen: 2 bottom, 3 top, 4 bottom, 5 bottom, 6 top and bottom, 7 top and bottom, 10 bottom, 12 top, 18 bottom, 19 bottom, 20 top and bottom, 21 top, 22 top and bottom, 23 top and bottom, 24, 25 top, 26, 28 top and bottom, 29 top, 30 bottom. Brydon Thomason: 8 bottom, 14 bottom, 17 top, 21 bottom, 27 top and bottom. Julie Wild: 13 top and bottom.

Drawing on page ii © Simon King.